Tears

Dinah O'Dowd was born and raised in Dublin. In 1959, at the age of 19, she escaped the suffocating atmosphere of Ireland, leaving her first born behind. It was at a pub she worked at in Woolwich that she met her future husband, Gerry O'Dowd. Over the years Dinah suffered repeated physical assault and prolonged mental torture, yet successfully bore and raised six children, one of whom became a world superstar – Boy George. In 2001 Dinah and Gerry finally divorced, after 42 years together. Dinah now lives alone in South East London.

Cry Salty Tears

Dinah O'Dowd

arrow books

Published in the United Kingdom by Arrow Books in 2007

3 5 7 9 10 8 6 4 2

Copyright © Dinah O'Dowd with Paul Gorman 2007

Dinah O'Dowd has asserted her right under the Copyright, Designs and Patents
Act, 1988 to be identified as the author of this work

First published in the United Kingdom in 2007 by Century

Arrow Books Limited
The Random House Group Limited
20 Vauxhall Bridge Road, London, SW1V 2SA

www.rbooks.co.uk

Addresses for companies within The Random House Group Limited can be
found at: www.randomhouse.co.uk/offices.htm

The Random House Group Limited Reg. No. 954009

A CIP catalogue record for this book
is available from the British Library

ISBN 9780099499787

The Random House Group Limited makes every effort to ensure that the papers
used in its books are made from trees that have been legally sourced from well-
managed and credibly certified forests. Our paper procurement policy can be
found at: www.randomhouse.co.uk/paper.htm

Typeset by Palimpsest Book Production Limited,
Grangemouth, Stirlingshire.
Printed in the UK by CPI Bookmarque, Croydon, CR0 4TD

This book is dedicated to my wonderful children – Richard, Kevin, George, Gerald, David and Siobhan – for their love and devotion. I also dedicate it to all my beautiful grandchildren and, of course, my sisters Annie, Phyllis, Cathy, Marie and Teresa, and my brothers Frank and John.

Acknowledgements

For their invaluable help in putting this book together, I'd like to thank Paul Gorman, Hannah Black, my sisters Phyllis, Cathy and Teresa, my son Kevin for his poem and George for his foreword.

Contents

Foreword
By Boy George

When Mum first announced that she intended to write a book about her life, I must admit I really didn't take her seriously. What could she possibly tell me that I didn't already know? I have always had a very open and honest relationship with my mother and from the age of thirteen, maybe younger, I was fiercely protective of her and would plead with her to leave my father who was violent and disrespectful and did everything he could to crush her spirit.

As a bratty teenager, I am ashamed to say that I started to think of Mum as weak because I couldn't understand why she stayed in such a destructive marriage. Once I grew up a bit I realised that Mum had stuck out the marriage for her kids and because she truly loved my father and believed in the sanctity of marriage. Dad was the one who went on about 'family loyalty' and blood being 'thicker than water', but he would also rage 'do as I say not as I do' and in the end it was that statement that rang most true.

The most shocking thing my father ever did was divorce mum forty three years too late after a secret relationship with a woman he went on to marry. No matter how bad my parents' relationships was, I always believed they would stick it out till the final breath. I was angry with Dad because I had begged him to give Mum a divorce and I hoped in vain that they could one day become friends.

It's always difficult to talk about Dad because he had some wonderful qualities and he could have been a great father and husband but his rage would always get the better of him and it was those close to him who suffered the most. Towards the end of his life he even became a bit 'spiritual' and was a qualified Reiki healer, but that didn't stop him being verbally abusive to Mum. For almost ten years it was as if he was leading a double life and his new friends and new family were lucky enough to enjoy the charming, intelligent side of Gerald O'Dowd, which we so seldom saw.

Dad's funeral was the final kick in the teeth for Mum (and for all of us) because she felt she was pushed to the side by Dad's new wife and denied the right to properly say goodbye to the man she had dedidated her life to. If I ever needed conformation that my mother was the greatest woman on earth, it was during those difficult weeks after my father passed away. A year later, Mum arranged a private family ceremony at our local church where a plaque was laid in Dad's memory. I was so moved and proud of Mum because I knew how hurt she was and once again had put her feelings to one side so that her children could say goodbye to their father.

Around that time I had a tearful conversation with Mum who was berating herself for sticking it out with Dad and in her words 'messing up my kids lives'.

It's true, the O'Dowds put the 'func' in dysfunctional and we have had more than our fair share of tragedy, but these days we are closer as a family than we've ever been.

Even though this book was at times difficult to read, it was also difficult to put down. Growing up, I was always very aware of my mother's suffering but there was clearly so much I didn't know and this book brought me to tears almost from the first page. It was terribly painful to read about my father beating my mother while she was pregnant with me and to learn that his three sisters and my grandmother did not come to her rescue. And hard to understand why her own father sent her back to a man he knew was beating and abusing her. Back then a woman became a man's property once he put a ring on her finger and so many women endured loveless marriages and years of abuse for the sake of their children.

All of us kids have added to Mum's grief over the years and I may be the biggest culprit of all. But no matter where I am in my life, at the top or bottom of the pop charts, I will only ever be one of Mum's six kids and I know we are all loved equally.

I was chuffed to learn that my dressing up was an inspiration and not just an embarrassment to Mum, because I remember her blocking the front door when I tried to leave the house in one of my freaky creations. When Mum realised I wasn't going to grow out of it she became a collaborator and would knock up whacky outfits on her sewing machine.

Even when fame went to my head and sent some of those close to me off the rails, Mum always managed to keep it together and would ground me with one of her deadpan Dinah-isms . . . The fur coat I bought her on a whirlwind trip to New York was 'A waste of money' and she quipped, 'Where am I going to wear that? To the bloody supermarket?' When I became vegetarian, though, I tried to get Mum to hand over that fur coat to a fur amnesty but she refused: 'That's my coat and I'll do what I like with it!'

Mum is fond of telling me that I'm too cynical and angry and she hates it when I get too graphic about my sexuality, but she is also refreshingly open minded and happy to tackle any subject. At times Mum can seem terribly old fashioned and prudish but just as quickly she can surprise you by saying something wilfully contradictory to spice up a debate. Recently, she was being interviewed for a documentary and was asked 'What do you think the neighbours thought of the O'Dowds?' She sat bolt upright and was clearly agitated, 'What sort of question is that? Why would you ask such a question?' she raged. 'I was never interested in what the neighbours thought, I never judged them and I never expected them to judge me or my family.'

It's that uncompromising spirit that makes me so proud of my mother and, even when times were hard and my father had gambled away all of the house-keeping, Mum always maintained her dignity and was never envious of what other people had. She dreamed of having a presentable home but it was never about impressing anyone else or keeping up with the Joneses. Mum has always had immense personal pride and inner strength and those qualities are what helped her survive this brilliantly documented journey.

Mum always said 'Women live longer because they cry'. So cry salty tears.

Boy George
London, 2006

Prologue

One day in 1962 I left south London, and took my three little boys Richard, Kevin and Georgie to my parents in Birmingham, escaping a violent and abusive husband who beat, kicked and berated me at every turn.

I was twenty-three, stick thin, without a friend in the world.

I'd finally had enough.

We turned up at my mother's door in Ladywood in torrential rain, like drowned rats. When I knocked at the house my sister opened the door and said, 'We don't want no pegs – go 'way!' and slammed the door in my face, thinking we were tinkers.

Soaked through, I hammered on the door, shouting, 'Kitty, Kitty, it's me!'

She opened up again, looked me over and cried, 'Oh quick, Mam, Mam, Mam, it's Dinah . . .'

My mother flew to the door and I blurted out, 'I've left him. I've left him!'

She got us all inside and tried to calm me. She dried me and fetched me dry clothes belonging to one of my sisters. We then warmed the kids and got them a drink.

'Where's their clothes?' Mam asked.

'I didn't bring anything with me,' I confessed, still shivering from fright and cold. 'I just ran. He was ranting and raving and I didn't want to be hurt again.'

'What do you mean?'

'He's hit me before, Mam,' I said. This was the first time I'd admitted it to my parents.

'Bastard,' she said. 'I'll kill him.'

But as my mother raged, my dad sat me down and said quietly, 'Now listen, chicken. You can't take the children away from their father.'

'I don't want to go back, Dad,' I said. 'I'm not going!'

He became angry, seemingly for no reason. He was the person I thought would stick up for me most in the world, but he didn't. Instead he said, 'I'm sorry, love, but they are his children and he has a right.'

When I tried to argue with him he just said, 'You've made your bed, now you must lie in it.'

I'll never forget that, nor the words my mother said to me later: 'You'll cry salty tears, my girl.'

She was right there. And how.

Chapter One

Dublin Through and Through

*Me, Phyllis and Marie on my
mother's knee, Dublin, 1949*

My father Francis Glynn was Dublin through and through. Known to everybody as Franco, he came into this world on 22 June 1914. His parents Richard, known as Dixer, and Molly Glynn were themselves Dublin born and bred and lived all their lives together in Dominic Street, about five minutes from where I was brought up, close to the city centre. Dad was one of five along with Dixer (named after his father), John, Sallo and Cissy. My nan also lost a daughter in childbirth, Annie, whose name was later taken by my eldest sister.

Grandad Glynn fought in the First World War and was awarded medals for bravery. When he died at the age of seventy-five in the mid-1950s his remains were taken to Kilmainham, which was once famously a jail but has been for many years a museum and an Irish national landmark.

When he came out of the army, Grandad was a jack of all trades; he could mend shoes, cut people's hair, make a coat. He was a very creative man, and was always immaculately turned out in a Crombie-style overcoat, Homburg hat, nails buffed, polished shoes. He also had beautiful feet, though I definitely don't take after him in that department! He was very much a family man and loved my granny. They were like Darby and Joan, the first old people I ever saw who would hold hands walking along the street.

Grandad always seemed to be cross with my dad, probably because they were like chalk and cheese in some respects but very alike in others, though Grandad wasn't such a drinker. He'd have a pint and then go home with a bottle for Molly and some pig's trotters. Even though she didn't have any teeth she managed to enjoy them. I remember very clearly Grandma's room, especially her big old bed with the brass knobs and inset ceramic balls I'd spin round as a child. At either end of the mantelpiece were two china dogs and on the wall hung a beautiful portrait of Michael Collins draped with the tricolour.

That generation witnessed the Troubles first hand; my mother's bridesmaid was only eighteen when she was involved in some crossfire and her arm was shot off by the Black and Tans. Even so, there wasn't any more of a Republican streak in my family than in most other Irish families. Michael Collins was a true patriot to Ireland, and having pictures of him didn't make you a member of the IRA. Although my grandfather had fought against the British in the Free State Army before he signed up, he wouldn't hear a word against the Brits. Nevertheless he still had this massive trunk where the Fenians hid when they were on the run after the Easter Rising of 1916, and in the basement of 75 Dominic Street a hole was cut so they could escape through the terrace and out via the building at the end, which housed the *Independent* newspaper.

To this day I am very, very proud to be Irish. Though I have spent most of my life in England, I still consider myself Irish, but I am not a fanatic. My parents and grandparents taught me that people should live and let live. I shall always be grateful to them for never preaching hatred of any sort.

My father was a stickler for the truth. You could do anything but lie to him. Whenever I was caught out for being naughty, I'd say, 'But you'll hit me . . .' And he'd say, 'As long as you tell me the truth, I won't.' And he wouldn't. He kept his word.

Growing up I felt very comfortable around my grandad. He told me fantastic stories, which I believed wholeheartedly, and consequently I got into trouble a few times in the playground and at school when I repeated them. He told me that when he was serving abroad he was all set to marry an African queen but decided against that course of action when he received a letter from Molly begging him to come back home.

I fell for it and told all my friends, but they just jeered. Grandad told me about faraway places and exotic fruit, making my mouth water. To me, the idea of travelling from our rooms in Wellington Street to South Africa was almost unimaginable, a quantum leap. When I got to travel forty years later – thanks to my son – it was the fulfilment of those childhood dreams inspired by my grandad.

My father was very handsome with green eyes and a mop of auburn hair – which he didn't bestow upon us; we all have thin fair hair. When he died at the age of fifty-three he didn't have a grey hair on his head. He was the apple of his mother's eye, as is so often the case with the rogue in the family. The other sons lived in lovely houses and they and their families were well dressed, while we rented rooms and were always poor. But they couldn't do what he could – decorate a hallway single-handedly, turn his hands to anything – so they'd always be down, saying, 'Franco, I want me front room done,' and off he would go. I remember once he papered our rooms at home and then meticulously placed these Regency borders he'd made to go around the pictures on the wall.

For a long time, Dad was a box maker for a bloke called Felix Lynch. Once Lynch offered him great things – a partnership in the firm – but the proviso was that my dad had to give up gambling. That was the one thing my dad couldn't do: forsake gambling. It was his weakness and he knew that sooner or later he would break that promise. Gambling is an awful thing. My father was a clever man, but unfortunately he couldn't always see the right road. His intelligence should have taken him much higher in life.

My mother was Bridget Margaret Keirnahan, and her family came from an area of Dublin known as the Gloucester Diamond, down by Summerhill. She was born in 1913, and was one of six, along with Dinah, Katie, Molly, Jack and William. We know very little about her parents, because she didn't know that much herself. Kiernahan is a popular name in Ireland and I haven't been able to trace her history and background. There is a very posh confectioner's called Kiernahan's in the centre of Dublin, on St George's Street, and I've heard word that there is some sort of family connection, but whether that is true or not has never been established.

My Grandma Kiernahan died in 1919 while giving birth to my mother's youngest brother, William. He was adopted and taken by his new parents to Australia, and my mother and her elder sister Dinah were sent to the Goldenbridge Convent in Inchicore, a suburb of Dublin. I still don't know what happened to Grandad Kiernahan, apart from the fact that he died not long after his wife. I don't know the cause. Maybe it was from a broken heart, but certainly it was felt that he couldn't cope, because the brothers and sisters were split up.

In all, my mother spent ten years in Goldenbridge, and didn't come out until she was sixteen. Her character was, I believe, carved by the horrors she experienced there. The nuns turned her into somebody who could not express love and emotion. She would never discuss what went on, but I know that the treatment meted out to her and the other girls damaged her for life. Mam was always very proper with us, and expected us to behave well. She could be quite cold, though often I put this down to the fact that she was so tired, working all the hours God sent.

We found out something of what she went through years later when my sister Phyllis saw a TV programme about the convent's history, which involved a lot of abuse.

Phyllis and I once tried to quiz our Aunt Dinah about life in the convent, but she would have none of it. 'They fed us, they clothed us and they educated us.' That was all she'd say, though she did reveal that Mam often had to wear a stained sheet around her neck because she wet the bed.

What skills would the nuns have had in showing affection to those poor children who had been taken away from their families? What do nuns know of a child's whims, wants or fears? You'd get the odd nun who had a caring streak but the majority of them didn't.

My mother must have blocked a lot of her early experiences out; she just didn't talk about it. A lot of people do that with periods of unhappiness. It's clear that whatever happens to you in your childhood affects the rest of your life. With guidance you can live with it and learn about it, but you can never quite come to terms with it, and I think that's true of my mam. Whatever happened in that place scarred her, though I think she must have had nerves of steel not only to have survived that but also to have later brought up a large family on very little money with an inveterate gambler for a husband.

When my mam first came out of the convent, her sister Molly – who was married by this time – took her in, and within three years she met my father. She took up the trade she had learnt in the convent, French-polishing, and worked at posh houses as a maid; he was a messenger for a butcher's at the time.

I remember we had a photograph of my dad when he was seventeen, a very handsome young man. I said to my Mam, 'Jeez, he was gorgeous.' He heard and said, 'Yeah, and look at me now. That's all her fault.' But, however much they rowed in their married life I always knew that my mother loved my father. He made her laugh, I think that was the main attraction. He was a very humorous feller, making up songs about things that had happened. They were hilarious. He had that knack of rhyming and I'm sure some of his talents emerged years later in our Georgie. Sometimes my mam would be a bit miserable about having no money, and he'd start her off laughing and soon we all would be.

They were respectable people, my parents. My mother wouldn't allow us to swear, not like the children today; she would be mortified if she heard us utter such words. She was always at us not to put our hands in our pockets. 'Ladies don't do that,' she'd say. 'Ladies don't whistle, ladies don't do this, that and the other.' I think if we'd had the finances we would have turned out a right bunch of snobs. My mother was very well spoken, didn't have a common Dublin accent, and when she called me, my mates would take the mickey, mimicking her voice: 'Dinah, Dinah . . .' I could row with her till the cows came home but I was always very defensive, wouldn't allow anyone else to say anything about her. That's when I showed my temper, and would go mad.

We're not sure how they met, but Dad probably delivered meat to a house where she worked. She had blue eyes and long dark hair, which she didn't have cut until she was fifty. They must have made a striking couple. When he was eighteen years old and she was nineteen they married in a little temporary chapel just off Sean McDermott Street in the Gloucester Diamond. My eldest sister Annie was born the following year, in May 1933. We think she may have already been in the tummy by the time they wed. Annie was followed by Frank a year later, and my other brother John – who died in April 2005 – in 1936.

My mam lost two babies, one before I was born on 23 January 1939 at the Rotunda Hospital in Parnell Square, just around the corner from where we all lived. Apparently I looked exactly like my dad when he was a kid, but as I get older I look increasingly like my mam. I can see her when I look in the mirror these days. I was christened Christina, but from the start was known as Dinah, a version of Tina. Us Irish shorten and change names all the time, and it happened to most of us, and a lot of the people we knew. What we are called is rarely the name on our birth certificate.

I remember the baby she had after me who only survived a few months. His name was William – we called him Wee-Wee, because he was so tiny.

My younger sister Phyllis (who was christened Philomena, see what I mean?) was born in 1943, and then Marie came along in 1946. Sadly she died at the age of twenty-three in the flu epidemic of 1969. Kathy – who's also known as Kitty – was born in 1948 while Teresa has always been the baby of the family, arriving four years later. Teresa was born with brittle bones, though that wasn't discovered until she fell at the age of one and broke her leg. She was in her first wheelchair at the age of three and has used calipers and sticks to get around all her life.

Teresa was definitely an accident. I clearly remember my parents proudly bringing her home in a hansom cab, wrapped in a tartan rug which I kept for years afterwards even though it was full of holes at the end. It always reminded me of that day when she first came home – I was jumping all over the place, so delighted to have a new baby sister.

So now there were ten of us crammed into the two rooms on the top floor of 11 Wellington Street, just five or so minutes from Dublin city centre, the old man gambling and drinking when he wasn't working, our mam having three or four cleaning jobs a day and all of us making ends meet.

Chapter Two

A Bit of a Timid Creature

Me squinting into the sun, with Marie, Annie and Phyllis, 1950

Of course, it's long gone now. Where we lived has been replaced with garages and on the other side there are town houses, but back then this was tenement living.

Outside our cold rooms, on the landing, there was a washstand and a bucket. The pail was our night-time toilet, to be taken down and emptied the next morning. Otherwise we had to go down the three flights of stairs to the lavatory in the yard we shared with the two other families who lived there. I would never go there. The kids in the house were mainly boys. Can you imagine the shame and embarrassment of waiting for the footsteps on the stairs and the possibility of somebody bursting in upon you at any time? I suffer from constipation to this day because of that.

The parlour on the ground floor was occupied by Mr and Mrs Carroll, who had eight children. Mrs Carroll was a moneylender. If you borrowed half a crown, the next week you had to give her it back with sixpence extra, making three shillings. If you borrowed five shillings, you'd have to give her an extra shilling back the following week. That was the way it was, and you knew where you stood.

She wasn't doing it for nothing but taking a chance on whether she'd see her money back at all, so it was only right that she charged.

In the two rooms on the next floor were another Mr and Mrs Carroll – not related – who had five or six sons, I don't recall exactly how many, and then there was us on the top floor. That means there were twenty-five or so people using just the one toilet. If you didn't clean it, nobody else would, because most couldn't be bothered. In the backyard was a rusty dustbin filled to the brim with rubbish. I grew to hate Wellington Street, because it was so crowded. I never seemed to have any space to myself.

The house was Georgian and our two rooms were massive, with a large front door and a round window-light above it. In the front room my parents' double bed faced the door, and next to that was a cabinet for the radio and record player my dad had made out of the rosewood he didn't sell when he broke our piano up because we couldn't afford to keep it. He also made a china cabinet, which was on the other side of the bed, next to the window. A curtain was strung up, behind which the clothes hung. In one recess in the front room was the fire with a large hearth which came out about three or four feet, and in the other was the cooker, with lidded buckets of fresh water next to it. There was another double bed in the front room, where Kathy and me slept.

Frank, John and Annie slept in the three beds in the back room, and when they married and moved out, me and the younger ones were all moved in there. The thing I hated most about sharing was that one of my sisters always wet the bed and it always seemed to be me lying next to them.

My mam was strict but I didn't appreciate how much she was struggling to make ends meet. She was very particular about her appearance, very clean and a bit of a snob, a woman with no money but she had ideas, if you know what I mean. My mother was forever cleaning; her thing was that cleanliness is next to godliness, instilled in her by the nuns, I expect. When you're little you don't mind being bathed but she insisted on doing it for as long as we lived at home. When you're in your early teens you don't want to sit in a tin bath in front of the fire being scrubbed mercilessly.

My dad liked a drink, and in the main he was a happy drunk, coming in merry of an evening. But what with his gambling as well, I was never attracted to alcohol and neither were the rest of us. My brother John and sister Annie didn't mind a tipple when they grew up but, like me, Frank was twenty-one before he had his first drop, which was quite unusual for a young lad in Ireland. His mates had all been away in England, and when they got back they took him out. I remember we were all in bed when I heard this crying. I went to the door and there was Frank, absolutely paralytic, with our neighbour from downstairs, Mr Carroll, who said, 'Frank doesn't want his mammy to see him like this.'

Frank literally couldn't put one foot in front of another. Soon we were all up and my dad said, 'What did ye want to go and do that to yourself for?' But throughout, Frank's only concern was that our mother didn't see him in that state. We got him to bed and no more was said, but he never was the worse for drink again.

One of my earliest memories is when we had these rabbits in a hutch in the yard. Things got hard and they had to be killed for food. We were all hanging out of the back window pleading, 'No, Daddy, don't, please don't!' Of course when the stew came round, we couldn't eat it, because they'd been our pets. But money was short and such things had to be done.

Back then, us kids weren't really aware of how hard life was. We may have been poor but we were never scruffy. I don't know where she pulled it from, but Mam always made sure we received something new at Easter, in August and at Christmas. Even if it was only a pair of plimsolls, socks or a ribbon, at least you had something you could go out in and show yourself off. I can remember us girls proudly wearing big balls of ribbon in our hair.

Birthdays weren't really celebrated. You certainly didn't get cards. I think I was married before I received my first birthday card. When Dominic Carroll from downstairs had his twenty-first, however, it was a different matter. No one had ever had a party like that. We were all there; I was about fifteen. It was held in a hall off Marlborough Street, and just us kids, no parents. There was food and a band. It was fantastic. There's a photo of Phyllis and me at it, having the time of our lives.

When it came to my mother, I was always trying to please her, scrubbing and polishing – 'I'll do that, Mammy' – but she never seemed to be satisfied.

I think now that the reason we clashed is that I am very much like her. She was a resilient person and coped with eight children almost single-handedly, and I went on to raise six kids in sometimes similarly desperate circumstances, as you will see.

As a child I loved my dad; he was the best thing since sliced bread to me. He was very tall, with hands like shovels. You wouldn't want to get a wallop off him twice, though he wasn't much of a one for that. The older ones had been brought up when my dad was much tougher; they saw things which I didn't. In fact my eldest sister Annie had no time for him at all, and couldn't wait to leave. Mother did most of the whacking, but sometimes when he was pushed by her, he would. But if you ducked and he missed he wouldn't try it again!

If my mam shouted, that was the worst thing because even though she found it hard to show love I loved her more than anything in the world. She could never hug me, and that's what I wanted most of all.

I wasn't a rowdy child; in fact I was a bit of a timid creature. Frightened of people with loud voices, I hated conflict and if my mam or dad were angry with each other or me I shook like a leaf. Of an evening, us kids would sit around on the steps of Wellington Street and tell ghost stories. Afterwards I'd be petrified as I went up the stairs to our rooms, mainly because I had a terrible fear of the dark. The tenement houses back then were gloomy, with very tall ceilings and lots of crevices and shadows. As you went into our hallway there was an arch with a recess, and sometimes the boys would hide there and jump out at you to give you a fright.

I don't know where that nervous side of me came from because, by and large, my childhood was a happy one. I'd be out playing with the other kids or visiting my nan in Dominic Street or my Aunt Molly's in Oliver Bonds.

I remember once running all the way home from Molly's so I wouldn't be late for tea. 'What have you got on your face?' my dad asked suspiciously. I had lovely rosy cheeks from running, but he thought I had put rouge on them. He hated make-up. 'See that lipstick?' he'd say. 'It's made out of monkey's blood, you know.' I was never really one for make-up anyway, so where Georgie gets that from I don't know. My mother might put a bit of lipstick on herself if she was going out, but that would be it.

We had lots of rules. For example, our mother wouldn't let us use soap on our faces because it clogged the pores, and sure enough none of us suffered from spots as teenagers. I don't remember my father washing his hair either. He'd say, 'If you're washing your hair every day you're washing the goodness out of it, all the natural oils.' There was definitely something in that because he had a fine head of hair all his life.

There were kids everywhere, and I had teems of friends: my best mate Hannah Lindsay lived next door to me and was one of twelve brothers and sisters. The boy who lived on the opposite side was also a pal, though he accidentally split my head open one day when we were tussling over a Doris Day picture. Down the road were my other friends, Phyllis Mulvey and Marie Geraghty. Mrs Geraghty had loads of children, I think as many as fourteen. They were all very handsome, as were another set of Geraghtys in Wellington Street, who all looked Mediterranean.

Even if someone fell out with you, there were plenty of other kids to play with. We'd be off to the playground up the Broad Stone, about five minutes away. That had a section for the smaller kids, a sandpit and the like, then there was an area where you could play rounders and a hut where the women used to come and teach the girls how to sew and knit. Meanwhile Dikey Carroll, the deaf husband of the lady who lived on the second floor of number

11, was ever so kind to us children, taking us away for day trips to Port Mannik.

We were always outdoors, playing in the street, racing each other around the block. My uncle worked at Guinness's, and brought us thick ropes which we used to make swings from the lamp posts. They were too thick for individual skipping ropes but sometimes the mothers would come out and grab each end across the street and you'd have fifty kids jumping up and down.

I wouldn't exactly describe life back then as rough. We all had similar dwellings, though families like the Lindsays had extra rooms to accommodate all the kids, and their furniture was grander than ours because so many of them were working. Their grandmother did the dinners at school, and because Hannah was my best mate I'd get the extra sandwiches they handed out every afternoon. It would be corned beef one day, cheese the next and jam the next, and then it would be back to corned beef. We'd also have a bottle of milk, though I'd maybe have two or three bottles a day from Hannah's nan, so I was well nourished. My first school was St Joseph's in Wellington Street where I went with all the other little ones. Then I went on to George's Hill, the convent run by nuns, where I stayed until I left at fourteen.

In a way, life was very innocent and I suppose I was quite childish. Even though things were difficult, there wasn't much crime or violence. The biggest job I ever heard of was when some of the boys stole a huge wedding cake off Kennedy's, the baker's van. Wellington Street was full of wedding cake that week; we were all eating it. God help the poor bride, whoever she was.

Of course there were gangs. We knew that the Northside didn't like the South, and vice versa, but they didn't impinge on our lives. I certainly wasn't in a gang and don't remember my two brothers being in one either.

The most mischief us kids got up to was playing tricks on the rag-and-bone man, Daddy Stein. In twos and threes we'd go to his yard in St Mary's Avenue and bring him a few jam jars; a little one went for a halfpenny and a big fat one a penny or maybe tuppence. While he was occupied with one of us, the others would be nicking the jars out of the box where he'd put them, washed and ready to go back to the factory. Then we'd sell them back to him. That might scrape fourpence each to go to the pictures at the Plaza round the corner. I went to see *Lassie Come Home* three times, twice with Dominic Carroll from downstairs. He took me because his beautiful sheepdog had died, and he was heartbroken, so seeing Lassie made him feel better.

We were blissfully unaware of the war, even though I was six when it ended. The only thing we knew about the fact that it was happening was the coupons introduced to deal with the shortages. Our mothers got their groceries for the week at Mrs Coffee's, and every Friday when our dads came home from work you'd be sent over to settle the bill, which had been itemised. I clearly remember paying with coupons a few times.

Of course on those occasions I never mentioned the packet of ten fags my brother John regularly persuaded me to get for him, so I would always be in trouble, because he would never reimburse me and the housekeeping would be short.

'Father, I don't remember buying those cigarettes for you on such-and-such a night,' my mam'd say to my dad as she went through the bill.

'No, I never had them then,' he'd respond.

'Well, who were these bought for?' she'd ask, and of course I'd get a wallop.

I can remember there were times when my mother didn't even get a wage to pay that weekly bill because my father was consumed by gambling: the gee-gees, the dogs, anything. Usually she would receive five pounds a week from him; his weekly pay would have been around seven or eight pounds at the time, for eight children. But that money would go and we'd be back the next week to buying everything on tick. He did come home with money he'd won occasionally. One Christmas morning after mass he took us all to Carroll's toyshop and we were allowed to pick what-ever we liked. He'd had a big win the night before.

When my old man came in and there was no money, my mother would be crying. But my eldest brother was very good. Frank was forever getting her out of holes. One day my mam was particularly desperate, so I soaked some old jumpers and then wrung them out, which meant that they were quite a weight when I put them in the bag for Daddy Stein.

'How many jumpers you got in there, then?' he asked. 'They're quite a load.'

I didn't answer and he gave me a shilling. But he must have known. He was well-to-do compared with us, and I'm sure he didn't mind us scratching a penny here or there.

When times were really tight it would be down to Mr Scully, who worked at old Mr Weaver's pawn shop. I brought things down there that would make you laugh: a coat of my dad's that he wasn't going to wear, a pair of sheets. You could pawn anything. I had a great rapport with Mr Scully so I could take anything over. I'd wrap the sheets up in brown paper and ask him not to open it. 'There's a little patch on one of them,' I'd say. 'I'll get them out on Friday.' You might earn half a crown for those. A lot of money in those days.

But if it was Weaver, he'd open the package imme-diately, see their condition and shout, 'Take this and get out of my shop! Don't let me see you again!'

A lot of people didn't like being seen visiting the pawn, so I'd go for them, and get sixpence which would go straight to my mam.

Money meant a lot to us. I remember the first time I went to a bingo hall years later with my mate Heather. I spent half a crown and was mortified. 'I could have bought a loaf of bread, a pound of butter and half a dozen eggs with that,' I said. 'God, it's only half a crown,' she said, but with my upbringing it was diffi-cult to dismiss spending that amount of money so easily.

Chapter Three

Oh Mammy, What Happened?

Mam and Dad in their back garden,
early 60s

Life was very different back then. When we played in the streets you'd be lucky if you saw two cars a day, and then they'd be those Austins – 'matchbox cars' we called them. The baker's van would come out of Kennedy's, but apart from that the streets were ours.

Glennon's the greengrocer's was on the corner of Wellington Street. Next to it was a lane and then a row of little houses going down to the pub. One lady there, Mrs Gorman, had a whole cottage to herself, which must have been fantastic, and next to her was Mrs Sheridan, who told fortunes with her crystal ball. She was lovely, a very pretty lady with beautiful white hair. My mam went to see her just the once, though I don't know what she told her since it wasn't the sort of thing my mother would have discussed. Around the corner in Dorset Street was a gypsy family, the Murphys, and many years later it turned out that one of my nieces married one of their grandchildren.

On the other side of Wellington Street was Kennedy's. When I was nine or ten, I ran errands for the men who worked the night shift there, nipping round the corner for them and getting an egg or a sausage or whatever and taking it to them for their breakfast. Of course they had all the bread they wanted and they'd give me a bag of hot doughnuts in return. At the end of the week you'd get sixpence off each of them, and some weeks I'd come home with three or four shillings. And, because I helped them, when the ovens were cleaned out I got first pick of the cinders. I would be waiting with my bucket and bring the cinders back for my mam. You would bank the fire up and then it would go for hours and hours.

There were loads of ways to earn the odd penny as I was growing up. I babysat for Kathleen McCullough, whose mam was the fortune-teller. Kathleen McCullough's husband Maxie was a boxer who travelled a lot, to the north and to England, and by the time I was twelve I was paid ten shillings a week for looking after her kids during the summer holidays.

You couldn't keep any of that money; all of it went

to your mam. Money was so scarce you needed every penny you could get your hands on.

Because my father made the boxes and crates for oranges, apples and other fruit and vegetables, he would sometimes go down to the country in the delivery lorries and come back loaded with food for all of us. The farmers would give them sacks and sacks of potatoes, carrots, cabbages, apples, pears. There might be a brace of pheasant, rabbit, hare, duck. It was fantastic.

We were lucky because my father was also a good cook; my mam was lousy, so he'd prepare some really tasty dishes when he came back from the countryside.

My dad would not allow a fry-up in our rooms. He insisted that everything we ate was grilled or baked, because he hated fried food. That didn't stop us having bread and dripping. Nan Glennon next door used to get buckets of dripping from the hospital. Stews were the big thing in our family. We had one nearly every day apart from the weekends when we'd maybe have a chicken.

When things were bad in Ireland, Dad would come over to England and find work, sending the money home. He was a while on the railways and also worked in a hotel, where he picked up a lot of his culinary skills.

He put them to good use. For a long time as a kid I would only eat fish from the fish and chip shop, until one day he made me soused mackerel, which I loved.

The main fish we all ate at the time was whiting, which we had every Friday. Years later, when I first arrived in England, I asked to buy some in a fish-monger's, and the guy said, 'Is it for the cat? We don't eat that here.' And then in the 1970s when the Cod Wars were on, it was only me that identified the 'white fish' being sold by our local fish and chip shop as whiting, because I was raised on that distinc-tive flavour.

I learnt how to cook liver when my mother was diagnosed as diabetic and was told that ox liver was one of the cheapest forms of counteracting its ill effects, as well as being one of the most nutritious. So I made that for her regularly, but the first thing I ever tried to make was a pie. I'd watched my mother put the flour and margarine and salt together to make the pastry, so one day on my own I cooked this pie and presented it to the family that evening. I wouldn't say it was a disaster but it wasn't a triumph either. My brothers were going, 'Hmm, it's a bit hard . . .'

While we were all growing up it was nothing for my mother to have three or four jobs at the same time, mainly cleaning for rich people. She also used her training as a French-polisher, going to beautiful houses to regularly polish their balustrades and pianos. I think that's where we got our appreciation of old furniture. We all love that craftsmanship. My father bestowed upon us a love of books. He educated himself and loved reading. I remember watching an episode of *University Challenge* with him many years later, and was astounded by the amount of answers he got correct.

My brother John was the same, reading everything he could get his hands on, though he was a totally different character to my dad. You could hear a pin drop around John, even though he had seven kids. If they were up to anything he would quietly call them over and say, 'I want a word . . .' There's no doubt his five boys and two girls had a very happy upbringing. I went to one of their weddings recently and all you could see was teeth. 'Have you noticed anything about John's children?' I asked Phyllis. 'Yes,' she said. 'They're always happy and they know what you're going to say because they're all very bright.'

I miss my brother ever so much but understand now that the way John lived his life as a father and husband was his reaction to the way we were brought up. He was very chilled and laid-back, not forthright like our dad, but liked things quiet and on an even keel. Frank, on the other hand, was boisterous. He was a real songbird and used to enter singing competitions all the time. He won a few as well. Frank had a fine voice, and I'll always remember the first time he saw George perform in concert. He said, 'You see I never had that – charisma. He's got the audience eating out of his hands, Dinah. I was too scared.'

If Frank and his mates wanted money, he just used to open his mouth and sing, and people would give them a few bob and they'd go off and have a great night. The peak of Frank's passion for singing was when he won the competition at Dublin's Theatre Royal two weeks on the trot. They asked him to carry on, but by that time he had a wife and two kids, and to go further would have meant giving up his job, so he turned down the opportunity. That's a shame because my mother would have been in her element. She was dying for him to be a star, maybe because that would have been such a contrast to her own existence.

I too loved singing as a kid. I was definitely going to be Doris Day when I grew up, that was my dream. And without dreams where are you? I'd play her records at home, but there was lots beside Doris Day being played in our house. My father liked all sorts apart from Frank Sinatra, who my mother loved. 'Ah, he messes about with songs,' my dad would grumble. 'He never sings it straight.' Years later, though, when Nancy Sinatra came out with 'These Boots Are Made for Walking', I was sat on a bus with him in Birmingham. He'd heard it just once on the radio and he sang every word, perfectly. The whole bus joined in. He'd do things like that, spontaneously.

When we all got together at number 11, my dad would sing songs like the old classic 'A Pal Must Be a Pal Forever', and my mother loved hearing Frank singing 'Danny Boy'. Often, us kids would have our own parties on the stairs at number 11. My big sister would gather us all together and we'd each sing a song. Of course mine would be anything by Doris Day, particularly 'Secret Love'. But I wasn't just a fan of hers. Because of the American connection with Ireland, everything coming over the Atlantic hit Dublin before it got to London, so we were up on all the new rock and roll stars. When Johnnie Ray and Guy Mitchell came along I loved them, even though, when you think of songs like 'She Wears Red Feathers' you realise they were a bit stupid. There always seemed to be some sort of gathering, and if somebody stood up you'd all be told to be quiet. 'Your man's singing,' they'd say, and even if he couldn't keep a note, the view was, 'At least he's trying.' There was a lot of encouragement.

Some of my grandmother's relations were very musical. Her sister married into a family called the Dargans, and they all played instruments. Aunt Kathleen played the drums, her husband played the piano accordion, another sister played the clarinet. They performed 'Ballin' the Jack' at my sister's wedding with Aunt Cissy and her best friend Betty on vocals doing all the moves, and it was brilliant.

As I say, you were encouraged in those days. When Mam had the money we'd go to Irish dancing lessons, and Marie – who had thick curly locks while the rest of us have very fine, flyaway hair – went to ballet classes. Meanwhile, poor old Kitty was mad about dancing. She'd come home from school, fling her satchel and coat down and start tap-tap-tapping away on the hearth, but she never got to go to any classes. Mother just couldn't keep up the payments, and couldn't afford the fancy costumes for us to enter any dancing competitions.

So we missed out on things, but we were pretty resilient. Though we were often hungry, we never starved. We had porridge every single morning but there was no food until the sandwich at school in the afternoon. I remember picking up an apple off the street on the way to school and eating it during a lesson. But no matter how tight money was, we'd have something every day, even if it was bread and dripping. Or we'd have what we called Mammy's stew – you know, hunt the meat! There'd be half a pound of mince in a massive pot with lots of vegetables. Whatever she fed us must have been good because none of us were undernourished or in hospital, apart from Teresa, but that was down to her condition. Lots of children we knew really went without. Once I came home at lunchtime and the only thing we had was an egg, which I shared with my sister. At least we were eating, and you savoured it.

There were some things we went without. I didn't see toilet rolls until I left Dublin in 1959. They existed, but my family couldn't afford them. Don't get me wrong, though. It wasn't an *Angela's Ashes* scenario, one of complete deprivation, and I'm not sure I believe some of the things in that book anyway. As I said, when my father came back from the country he was loaded down. Mother would borrow my granny's massive cauldron and in it would all go. She would share that stew with neighbours and friends, because we helped one another.

Even then I realised what a hard grind it was for

my mother. She would be up and out every morning at six o'clock. Because I was always trying to please her I'd be the one making the porridge for the family, and anyway by the time I was fourteen Annie had married and moved out so it was down to me to look after the little ones because Frank and John weren't expected to pitch in. In fact my brothers, like most boys, got away with murder; they didn't have to do anything. All the work and skivvying was down to us girls. That's not to say that they wouldn't occasionally help out; our Frank in particular would sometimes muck in.

We stopped washing ourselves in the tin bath in front of the fire when we discovered the local baths down off the Quays; I would take the little ones down there of a Saturday morning. For just sixpence I'd make sure we were all bathed.

The attendant would shout, 'Don't lock that door!'

But I'd say, 'I'm not getting undressed if there's a chance of somebody coming in.'

'Well as long as those other kids don't get in that bath . . .'

So I'd promise that they wouldn't and then tell them to be quiet and wash them each in turn, trying to stop them splashing about. The baths were huge; you could probably get about ten in them comfortably, so in we'd all go and then I'd clean it off with the disinfectant provided, ready for the next bunch.

We'd also take our washing down to the baths, to

the large rooms which had huge dryers, or we'd bring it to our mam's sister Molly, who took in people's washing as well as worked for Guinness's. She had twenty-one kids, though seven of them died when they were really young, and was a massive woman, a real Mother Earth character. If you were in trouble you talked to Molly and she'd sort you out.

The story went that Molly's husband used to arrive home every evening and the food would be on the table for him and the kids, but nothing for Molly. 'Oh, I had mine earlier,' she'd say. Finally her husband asked the children, and they said, 'No, Mummy doesn't eat her dinner,' because she was so preoccupied with making sure everyone else was fed. So from that day forth he insisted that she sit down and share his meal. I thought that was fantastic.

I loved Aunt Molly; she was such a warm character, and so different from my mam. First off she lived in rooms in Summerhill, which was close by, and then they moved to the Oliver Bond flats. The difference between rooms and a flat was that the latter had a toilet out the back and a bath. I remember the first time I had a proper bath, at my Aunt Sal's. It was in the kitchen, and, with a board over the top, it constituted the table you ate off as well.

As I say, we were very innocent; at the age of fourteen I was still playing kiss chase, and that wasn't unusual for girls then. It was at that age that I got my first period. I was at the cinema and went to the toilet and thought, 'Oh my God, what's this?' As an

adolescent I wasn't very well developed. I'd have hated
to have got them at eleven or twelve like some of the
girls because I was still a child then, not very streetwise. My next thought was, 'How am I going to tell
my mam?' So I waited until there was only me and
her in the room and then hitched up my skirt accidentally on purpose and let her see what had happened
when I went to step up on a chair, pretending to get
something from the top of the wardrobe.

It was then that she said, 'Dinah get down. Come
into the back room. I want to talk to you.' In there
she said solemnly, 'I've got something to tell you.
You've now got your monthlies, and have to put clean
things on regularly. This means you can't be with
boys. Don't let any boys touch you or get near you.'

And that was it. No mention of periods or why
these bodily functions had started or why I mustn't
let boys get near me. Condoms or any form of protec-
tion certainly weren't discussed. Even though my
parents weren't strict churchgoers, the Catholic
Church ruled Ireland with a rod of steel, and contraception was not only a sin, it was illegal.

From that day, if a boy caught me when we played
kiss chase and I was on my monthlies, I screamed the
place down: 'Get off me, get off me! You're not
allowed to touch me.' My mates used to laugh at me:
'What's the matter with you?' I suppose I must have
thought that I'd have a baby if I let them touch me.
We weren't grown up at all.

Sex wasn't something you talked about, not even

with your friends. You said you had your monthlies, and that was an end to it. Everybody hated them but we didn't discuss it further than that. I certainly didn't talk about it with my parents or my elder sister Annie. In fact, she was even greener than me and when she was twenty she was still expected to be back at home by ten o'clock, even though she was courting the man who became her husband. And now they've been together over fifty years. But back then I can clearly remember my mother calling her up, even though she was only standing chatting at the front door. Annie used to get dressed and undressed in the wardrobe, she was so frightened that any of us would see her naked. Even when she was married, I later found out, she continued to do that!

The amazing thing was that, later on, in the 1960s when my parents lived in Birmingham, my younger sister Kathy was allowed to stay over at her boyfriend's. 'But she's only twenty!' I told them. 'Well times are different now Dinah,' was all they said.

When I was fourteen an incident occurred after which, I'm afraid, I lost respect for my father. I had just suffered acute appendicitis, and was sent to convalesce for two weeks at Fairy Hill in Dublin. These days they send you home the same day after an appendectomy, but then it was very different. My scar is so long that once, when I was being examined during a pregnancy by a doctor, he exclaimed, 'My God! What the hell is that?'

I'd been at Fairy Hill a while when, early one

morning, I don't know why, I said to them, 'Could I go home now? I need to see me mam.'

'What are you talking about?' said the nurse. 'You're off next week as it is.' But I was insistent and they relented.

I took the train home, arriving late morning. As I walked to the top of the stairs, I saw the front door was off its hinges. There it was, on the floor. And there was my mam, sitting up in bed, absolutely black and blue.

I ran to her, crying, 'Oh Mammy, what happened, what happened?' I'd never seen anybody that battered before. She had bruises all over her face and arms. She couldn't move one of her hands from where she'd tried to protect herself.

'Where's Daddy?' I asked, and then saw him, lying on the floor in a heap, passed out from the drink.

Apparently the night before they'd been out at Mooney's. My mam was wearing a tam-o'-shanter and this bloke kept on annoying her by snatching it off her head. At the same time as he was bugging my mam, the feller was feeding my dad drink; my father was a great ring player, an Irish pub game which involved metal hooks and rings, and had quite a following in Dublin, and this bloke was chivvying him along. When my mother started complaining about the guy, my father grew upset. He wanted her to keep shtum so the drink would keep flowing, but my mam wouldn't be silenced. Evidently, by the time they got home, my father was so enraged that my mother had had a go at this bloke, he gave her a terrible beating.

The sight of her in that bed is a picture I will never forget. Even though she and I fought like cat and dog through my teenage years, I couldn't bear to see her in that state. And the immediate loss of respect for my father – at his lack of self-control, at his bullying nature, at his cowardice – was something that would stay with me for the rest of my life.

Chapter Four

I Could Sleep on Glass

Marie, Phyllis and Cathy outside number 11, 1959

At the age of fourteen I took a job in a shoe factory in Berkeley Road at one pound five shillings a week, putting glue on the uppers. I gave all my wages to my parents, apart from half a crown.

Before I came home that first Friday, I lost my very first week's pay on a slot machine. They were all the rage and in all the shops. When I shamefacedly explained what had happened, my dad marched me back to the shop where I'd lost the money and demanded they return the cash, because I was underage.

When the feller refused, my dad picked the slot machine up and said, 'Either you give me the money or this goes on the floor and I'll take it out of that.

Or we can call the police. You shouldn't have allowed her to play it.'

The bloke handed over the money and on the way back I swore I would never go back there. And when I got home I received a wallop. 'What possessed you to do such a thing?!' yelled my dad.

All I could say was, 'I don't know, Da. First of all I was winning . . . and then I wasn't.' He should have known all about that experience.

I resented giving my parents the majority of my wages, because music and dancing were my great passions and on half a crown I couldn't really afford to go to as many dances as I would have liked. This made me become a bit of a rebel, always questioning them, always answering back.

One time I arrived home from work to find a crowd gathered outside next door's and our neighbours hanging out of the first-floor window, the wife in floods of tears. At the centre of the crowd was one of her sons, mercilessly beating his wife. I'll never forget screaming, 'Stop, stop, stop. He's hurting her, he's hurting her!' But nobody intervened. The view was that, when it came to a married couple, you didn't interfere. That event stayed with me. I have never been able to understand why a man feels the necessity to hit a woman for no reason. When it was over I was sobbing to my family, 'Why didn't you stop it? Why didn't his mother stop him?' And why didn't she? Fear, I suppose.

The other thing you heard about, and this made

me question religion, was blokes coming home from the pub on a Saturday night, bashing their wives and then going to church all contrite the next morning. How could God condone that? This was just one of the conflicts in my mind as a teenager.

I hated being restricted and hated the way, in Ireland, you were thought of as 'wild' if you liked going out and dancing. My mother would always say, 'There's no good on the streets after ten o'clock.'

I could never understand why I wasn't allowed to stay out late. I was indignant when told to be home by eleven o'clock. 'Why? Hannah and Marie stay till the end of the dance, Mam, so why can't I?'

'Well, I'm not their mother and you're not Hannah Lindsay so you can come home at eleven or you're not going out any more.'

This was the era of dance halls. They were all over the place, and only five minutes down the road in O'Connell Street I'd go to the Ballerina or the Olympia. The showbands played rock and roll hits by the likes of Bill Haley and the Comets, or we would go to hops to dance to the records themselves. Hops were always cheaper and were held everywhere and anywhere. Somebody would set up their record player in a garage; you'd pay your sixpence and dance the night away.

There was no alcohol and, when I think about it now, I'm amazed that we got so much fun out of dancing. In fact, I didn't drink alcohol until I was twenty-one, when I had a gin and orange and didn't like it at all. Around the age of fifteen I started to smoke, though I was never allowed to do that indoors, and I felt as though I was gaining my independence for the first time.

Then my mother took very ill and collapsed in the street. It was thrombosis, though she was only in her early forties. When she didn't come home we were all sent out to look for her and discovered that whoever found her had rushed her to the Mather Hospital by cab. That was the only time I ever saw my father cry. Thank God she lived. But the thrombosis was down below, and that's where she developed cancer years later.

While she was recuperating, my brother Frank, who was then twenty-one, took over the finances. My father wasn't allowed anything from the housekeeping. I can remember hearing him plead, 'Ah, Frank, come on. Give us a lend of two bob would ya?'

'No, Father. You've got your money. This is Mother's.'

During the time my mother was in hospital, Frank cleared all her debts. She didn't owe a penny to nobody and when she came out weeks later he was able to hand her notes, not coppers. Of course, what did she do? The following Thursday she lent Dad a pound, followed by another, and soon enough the gambling had got us back to square one. At the time I didn't understand or appreciate the situation, but I do now. I married a gambler, and know that they can lose the shirt off their back and expect you to come up with another. I have enormous respect for my mother for putting up with that and bringing us all up. She couldn't display affection but showed she loved us in so many other ways.

My mother died from cancer in February 1980 at the age of sixty-seven. She had been living with Phyllis and then moved to a hospice. That day I was a wreck. Our mother had been very cold towards us as children, never cuddling or kissing us nor, for that matter, showing any signs of physical affection. In fact she was always the one administering punishment for our childish misdemeanours, hitting and slapping us at every turn. It was difficult for me as a very sensitive child to square that with the fact that she really did love us, and I guess my tears stemmed from that fact. My sisters said to me, 'Why are you crying like this, Dinah? She beat the shit out of you when we were kids. You didn't get along.' But it just tore at me. I didn't want her to go because there was too much I wanted to say to her, and I knew then I was never going to get the chance. It was too late.

Back in 1954, my life was about to change forever. At one of the dance halls on Dorset Street I met a boy, Seamus. It was the usual night at the dance hall: all the girls over here and all the fellers over there, all of us eying each other up. He came over and tapped me on the shoulder and asked me for a jive. After dancing with him all night he walked me home.

Seamus wasn't that tall, about five feet four inches, which was great because I hated them too tall. He was a natty dresser and very handsome, with a thatch of blond hair. That night the verdict from the girls was that Seamus was a good-looking feller, though neither me nor any of my friends had seen him before. He said he knew me by sight, and came from a place called Whitehall. That was just a bus ride away from Wellington Street, but at the time we all stuck to our own little patches. Seamus was a bit more streetwise than me. He was working, after all, as a painter and decorator, and was a bit more out in the big wide world. He was a charming lad, and made me laugh.

So Seamus and I started going out, and within a few months I brought him to our rooms to meet my parents. Even though they knew we were going steady they still avoided discussing the facts of life or giving me any warnings. I also still had to be in by ten o'clock.

We saw each other for two years, but in all that time I never met his parents. I thought it was strange, especially when he told me that one of his brothers was to be married and I wasn't invited. I'd ask him if I could meet his parents: 'You've met my mam and dad, so why can't I meet yours?'

'I'll take you up one day,' he said. It never happened, yet I was happy to go along with what he wanted.

However, I did go to his place just the once, on a Sunday night.

It was very dark and there was nobody else in. His explanation was that they always kept it that way because his mother suffered from a condition which made her eyes sensitive to bright lights. It was all very odd, but when you're that age and you're in love everything else is obliterated. You don't see anything else; just you and that person who is the focus of your attention.

Then, about a year after we started seeing each other, out of the blue and for no reason at all, Seamus hit me, gave me a slap.

Earlier that evening I'd been at the bus stop chatting to my cousin Maureen, on my way to meet him to go to the pictures. We let one Whitehall bus go past because there was plenty of time; I didn't have to meet him till seven, and we were having a good conversation. Apparently his sister was on that bus and told him that she'd seen me talking to somebody.

Anyway, I caught the next one, and was still in time, arriving just before seven o'clock. I could tell he was in a bad mood. 'Why are you late?' he demanded unreasonably. 'Who was that you were talking to at the bus stop?'

I told him it was my cousin and asked what the problem was, and he suddenly lashed out at me.

'What was that all about?' I cried, and started to run. He caught up with me. 'I don't want to see you anymore,' I said. 'You can't slap me about. Who do you think you are?'

Of course he was really sorry, and swore he would

never do it again. As I was to learn, you get these warning signs, but you don't heed them because you want to think the best of the people you love. That night he talked me round, and we went to the pictures. Seamus had never shown any sign of violence towards me before, though by that time I had found out he had a bit of a reputation for it among the lads.

A few months later he stood me up one evening. I decided: 'That's it. I'm not going out with him no more.' Later on that night I was standing with a group of four or five friends on the main road down from Wellington Street when he drove past on the back of his brother's motorbike.

What I didn't see was the bike stop down the road and him get off. He came back after me. 'I wanna talk to yer,' he said.

'Well I don't want to talk to you,' I said. 'Go 'way.' With that he grabbed me and slapped me again, in front of my friends.

I flew up Wellington Street yelling that I was going to get my brothers. Of course he was faster than me, and soon caught up. He grabbed me again. 'Please, please, I'm really sorry, I just want to talk to you . . .' All that old crap. But I kept it up and told him I didn't want to see him anymore. And I didn't, not for a few weeks, though I didn't tell my brothers what had happened.

The two incidents where Seamus hit me weren't like the abuse I was to suffer at the hands of my husband later on, I want to make that plain. This was the 1950s, and this was the way men, particularly callow young lads in Dublin, behaved. Women were second-class citizens and if men thought you were out of line, they lashed out at you. I wasn't scared of Seamus, that was the big difference.

Seamus and I had been having sex with each other for quite a while by this stage, even though I didn't understand anything about it. We hadn't had any kind of sex education, from our parents or at school. For a girl like me, when you gave yourself to a man for the first time, you wanted to believe that it would be forever. Men didn't, and don't, think like that. So, as much as I didn't want him hitting me, I wanted to be with him and soon we started seeing each other again.

One weekend he was travelling to Manchester with some friends to watch a football match, and invited me along. Like an idiot, I packed a case but didn't tell my parents what we were up to as they would never have let me go.

We caught the boat and when we got to the station in Manchester it was lashing it down, miserable and grey. If this was England, I didn't like it one bit.

'Now, we have to go somewhere,' he announced, sitting me down with my case on a railway bench. 'You stay here and I'll see you later.' I didn't question him but remembered to ask for my ticket, which he gave me.

I must have sat there, all on my own, on that damp, cold platform, for three hours, watching the hands of the station clock slowly move. Then I saw on the departures list that there was a train going back to the boat, so I got on it and went back home.

When I arrived at Wellington Street, my dad asked where had I been and I told him. 'Seamus and his mates went off and didn't come back. I don't know what happened to them,' I said. 'All I did was stare at the station clock for hours on end.'

My dad was kindly. 'So you went all that way just to look at the time?' he joked, and that was an end to it.

But I continued to see Seamus, and it wasn't long before I fell pregnant. I told him my suspicions when my period stopped and I knew for sure when I asked a lady who lived across the road from me. I can't remember her name now, but she was very sympathetic and told me that I was definitely going to have a baby. 'Try not to worry, but you have to tell your mam and dad,' she said. Of course the fear and terror of how my parents would react was uppermost in my mind.

It was at this time that my mam took ill and was hospitalised. I was looking after the house and one day had to do a massive wash. This meant putting the huge tin bath on the stove, filling it with water, turning the gas on and heating it, taking it off and putting it on the table, topping it up with cold water and then washing and rinsing all our clothes, bed linen and cloths.

Although I was a tiny little thing, I was quite strong,

so I completed that, put the washing out on the line and over the cooker and went to the hospital to visit my mam. I sat by the bed and told her I had done the washing and cooked food for the rest of them.

'Good girl,' she said.

There was a pause and then I said, 'You know what, Mammy? I could sleep on glass.' That's all it took, and that's all I said. I was physically exhausted all of the time and for no apparent reason; my mum just put two and two together.

Two days later she was out of the hospital and she sent all the kids out and her and my dad sat me down. 'Go on, ask her,' she said to my father.

'I'm going to ask you something, chick, but don't tell me a lie,' he said to me.

I was petrified. In my head my voice was yelling, 'Oh God, Jesus, they know, they know . . .'

My dad said, 'Now don't be scared. Nothing's going to happen to you.' And I believed him; I did trust my father. 'Is there anything wrong with you?' he asked.

'What do you mean?' said I. Talk about green.

'Well, now, OK, how am I going to put this?' he said. 'Have you done something you shouldn't have done with Seamy? Has something stopped?'

I nodded my head once.

'You realise what's wrong with you?'

'No.'

'You're going to have a baby.'

Then I told him I knew, that I had asked the

neighbour and she'd confirmed it and that Seamus knew as well.

'What's he going to do about it?' my dad asked. I didn't know for sure, but Seamus seemed to be willing to take on the responsibility with me and had said he'd marry me.

A few days after the talk with my parents, Seamus came to see my priest with me at Berkeley Road, and I went with him to Whitehall to see his. The banns were put up. It wasn't going to be a white wedding, more one of the shotgun variety, and my sister Annie said that once we were married we could stay with her in one of the rooms at her house in Finglas. She had three bedrooms but already had kids, so said we could have the parlour. Even though it was a tiny room, I started to buy things for it and also the baby which was on the way.

I assumed he'd told his parents, but never asked. Ever since I had found out I was pregnant I'd been living in a twilight zone, unquestioning, not taking anything on board. It didn't seem to be real life. I knew it was happening, but I wasn't there. I was very frightened but numb. What worried me most was that I'd never been part of his family, so how would they take to me under these circumstances?

Although the banns had been put up, a date hadn't been arranged. I was around four months gone, and we were hoping to get the wedding set soon, when, one evening, Seamus didn't turn up to a meeting we'd arranged with my priest. He didn't turn up the next evening either, nor the one after that. Suddenly I couldn't get hold of Seamus, or find him anywhere, not in any of his haunts or with his friends. When I asked around, everybody clammed up and said they hadn't seen him. I asked my mam, still totally inno-cent, 'What do you think has happened to him?' I won't tell you what she said, but you can imagine.

With five months to go before the birth of our baby, Seamus disappeared off the face of the earth. Or from the streets of Dublin, at least.

Chapter Five

No Bed of Roses

Me (second left) and my friends just before I met Seamus, 1953

Deep down in my heart I knew what Seamus was up to, and I remember saying to my dad, 'You know, Daddy, I don't mind if he doesn't want to marry me.' Seamus was a year older than me – just eighteen – so both of us were only kids. I couldn't hate him for going on the missing list.

'Well, let's not talk like that,' said my dad. 'Let's see if we can find him. We'll go and see his parents.'

I begged, 'You won't fight with them, will you, Dad?'

He said calmly, 'No, no, no. We'll just go and find out what's going on.'

So off Mam and Dad went. I was left fretting at Wellington Street. When they returned I found out that, unfortunately, my mam hadn't been able to keep her mouth shut and it had turned into a big argument. The message came through loud and clear: Seamus wasn't willing to marry me and had gone to live with his brother, we didn't know where.

My dad had said to them, 'Would he not have the guts to come and tell her himself?' They told him that wasn't going to happen. Lucky for him, really, because if my dad had caught up with him he would have broken his neck. My father would never have forced us to marry each other, but there was a principle here. Seamus had broken his word to me.

When they came back and told me, I cried and cried. I started going into any local church to find the statue of St Jude, the patron saint of hopeless causes, and pray to him. I asked St Jude again and again why Seamus had done this to me, and pleaded with him to make Seamus come back.

While I was praying to St Jude, my dad decided to take action and visited a solicitor. 'Well, if he doesn't want to marry you, we don't want him to marry you either,' Dad said. 'But he has a child on the way which he must support.'

So they took Seamus to court for maintenance. My parents could have insisted he pay right up until our child was sixteen, but instead they settled for a sum of money, not a great deal. To raise a child over several years it had to be stretched, believe you me.

By the time the case was settled I'd set my heart

and decided I never wanted to see Seamus again. Once I knew that my mam and dad were going to stand by me, I was fine. I accepted my lot and didn't make a fuss about it – I licked my wounds and had a little cry and that was that. Unlike many pregnant teenagers in Ireland in the 1950s and '60s, there was never any prospect of a Magdalene Sisters scenario – of me being sent down the country and being forced to give up my baby. That was the era when most girls had to give their babies up for adoption if the father wasn't around, but my family stood by me.

Suddenly I was out of the twilight world, and couldn't wait for the baby to come even though my mother's constant warning was, 'This isn't going to be a bed of roses, you know that?'

I already knew that from the reaction of our neighbours. I remember going to the sink on the landing to get some water one day. As I filled the kettle, I heard Mrs Carroll down below say, 'Hey, did you hear about your woman upstairs? She's only pregnant.' Underneath the sink was our bag of spuds. So I picked up a potato, ran downstairs and flung it at her door, scarpering before she opened up. My mam heard the kerfuffle and asked me what was wrong. I told her that Mrs Carroll had been talking about me, and she said, 'Just ignore them. Take no notice.'

But still I couldn't shake the shame. I locked myself indoors and would only leave the house to pick up my money from the labour exchange. I even bought myself a big loose coat so nobody would see that I was showing. My friends knew, but I concealed myself from everybody else.

I think you carry shame, and I certainly did even though my mam and dad had accepted the situation. It helped that I had a family around me who all loved me and were willing to help. When my baby Richard was born, the younger ones were told they had a new brother, but the older ones knew he was mine. He became part of a family that was supportive and caring.

On the day Richard was born, 27 September 1957, both of my brothers had come home for their lunch. I had this pain in my back and must have winced as I moved around to ease it, because Frank asked, 'Are you OK? Why do you keep on moving like that?'

When I told him that I didn't have any pain in the front, but a 'funny feeling' he said to my mam, 'You'd better get her to the hospital.'

I remember lying in the labour ward and asking a nurse why all the other women were screaming so much. 'They're having their babies,' she told me.

'Well, I'm not going to scream,' I said.

'Good girl,' she said as she left to attend to another woman.

A few minutes later, I remember turning on my side, grabbing hold of the bar of the bed and pushing for all I was worth. I don't know why I did it; this urge just came over me. By the time the nurse had run to my bed, Richard was out.

'You naughty girl,' she exclaimed. 'You mustn't do that on your own!'

I started crying. 'What's the matter? What have I done?'

'Hey, all right, don't cry,' she soothed. 'You've had a little boy.'

That's how easy it was, and all my children were exactly the same. Apart from when Gerald was born in 1963, I never had a problem with any of their births.

Over the next couple of days all my friends came to see me, bringing little gifts. When Richard was four days old my parents were sitting by my bed with one of my sisters when a matron came in with some documents. 'Well, Mr Glynn, are you ready to sign this paper?'

My dad asked what it was. 'It's for the mother and baby to go to the Sacred Heart Convent in Drumcondra.'

When he asked why, she said, 'Surely to God you're not bringing this child home, born out of wedlock? Wouldn't it be best to have him put up for adoption?'

My dad, his voice rising in anger, said, 'Have you asked the mother whether she wants her baby adopted?'

'We don't have to ask the mother,' said the matron. 'I'm asking you.'

So my dad said to me, 'Do you want to keep this baby, Dinah?'

'Yes, Daddy, I do.'

'We won't be signing any papers,' he told the matron.

'Well,' she huffed, 'I've never heard anything so ridiculous in all my years.'

As the matron flounced out, my mother wasn't so certain. 'Do you think we're doing the right thing, Frank?' she asked him.

'Of course we are,' he said. 'One more mouth isn't going to break the bank, is it?'

Although I didn't understand what I now had to do, I was happy and felt secure in the love of my family. My mother had to show me how I could use the bottle rather than breastfeed him, everything. As a matter of fact, she took him over. She mothered Richard herself and my dad absolutely adored him. He'd come in of a night and take his cap off and put it on Richard's head and dandle him on his knee, chatting away to him.

One day a girl knocked at the door. She asked if I was Dinah Glynn, and if I had a baby. She told me her friend was going out with Seamus, and wondered whether she could see the baby. She didn't give a reason and I didn't ask; I was such an innocent that I invited her in, though now I believe she was in fact Seamus's new girlfriend and had decided to come and see Richard for herself. Seamus was probably waiting down the road for the verdict.

I told her that he looked like his father, Seamus. Richard was asleep in one of the big drawers of the chest in my room; we didn't have carrycots in those days. When she took a look she gasped, 'Oh God, he's very much like him, isn't he?' To this day, I don't know whether they doubted that Richard was his or if Seamus had been claiming he wasn't the father, but at that moment my mother came into the room.

'Who's this then?' she asked suspiciously.

'Oh, this is a lady who works with the girl who is going out with Seamy now,' I said, innocence itself. 'She's come to see the baby.'

'Ah, has she now?' said my mother, before turning to her. 'You. Out! Now!' As the girl fled, my mother said, 'What is wrong with you, girl? You're as soft as a brush!' I couldn't see why she was so angry. I didn't think badly of people, and if she wanted to see my baby, why not?

I only met Seamus one more time, not long after that visit. I was pushing the pram down Frederick Street after visiting the chemist's and he came over and asked whether he could see the baby.

'No! Go 'way,' I spat. And he did. He never again made any attempt to see the child and neither did his parents, sisters or brothers. In the years since I've often wondered at that. Didn't his parents want to know how their grandchild was, what he was like? They lived in the same city, just a bus ride away. Why did they never acknowledge his existence? Whatever his father and I had done, Richard was the innocent party. But at the time it didn't bother me because Richard was in such a loving environment. My dad adored him and Mam called him 'son'.

That was the last time I ever clapped eyes on Seamus. If he's passed me the times I've been in Ireland – and it is a small place, you're forever bumping into people you know – I haven't recognised him. Apart from maybe once, just a couple of years ago, when I was with Phyllis, getting into a cab in Dublin, and the people getting out were this older man and some-body who looked like his granddaughter. He greatly resembled Seamus, his blond hair long turned white, though he was maybe a shade too tall.

'Sure, that's him,' exclaimed Phyllis.

'Yeah, you might be right,' said I, but I'm still not certain.

And the funny thing is, even thinking about him now, he means nothing to me. Once Seamus did what he did, I lost all feelings for him and cut him out of my life completely.

I told Richard when he was eleven years old that my husband Gerald wasn't his father, that Seamus had deserted us both before he was born. As you'll see as my story unfolds, Richard arrived in London to live with us and the rest of our kids from Ireland when he was seven and he has always been treated as a full family member because he is. But with hind-sight, I wonder whether he was at too young an age to take the information on board. I don't know if he quite took it in at the time. My husband Gerald had always said that he would legally adopt him, but never did. Then when Richard was fifteen, without my knowledge, Gerald took him to one side and told him that he wasn't his father.

To this day I don't understand why Gerald did that. If he'd said to me, 'Listen, I think we ought to both talk to Richard about this,' that would have been fine. But he couldn't keep his tongue and told the other boys at the same time. This time it did have an effect on Richard. He hadn't quite left school, and started to get into a little bit of trouble. I told my daughter Siobhan when she was fourteen. I sat in the front room of our house in Shooter's Hill and cried, but she was fine about it. 'He's still my brother,' she said.

I think back now to Richard's father and still can't work out why Seamus behaved the way he did. I don't know whether he was influenced by his sisters and his parents. They lived in a house while we lived in rooms, so maybe we weren't far enough up the pecking order for them, but they weren't any different from me, my family or anybody else in Dublin at the time. My home was spotless and, as I say, my mother was a stickler for cleanliness. We may not have had grandeur but we had comfort.

Seamus was a coward, there's no doubt in my mind about that. If he had faced me and said, 'Look I'm too young to marry,' I would have cried but understood. That would have been far preferable to him running away.

But now, the way things turned out, I'm glad he did what he did. And he has missed out on a wonderful kid. I asked Richard if he ever wanted to find his father, and he always said, 'No. The truth is, Mam, he didn't want to know me, so what good would it be?'

Chapter Six

You Can Stick Your Job

Richard with Mam outside Wellington Street, 1958

No matter how much I argued with my mam during that period of my life, she was tremendous. Even though the nudge nudge, wink wink would go on as I wheeled my baby down the street, she gave me all her support and was never ashamed of me. But still I felt the shame myself, walking out with the pram and everybody looking at me, knowing that I had an infant but didn't have a husband. It wasn't the done thing, especially in the 1950s and particularly in Ireland. I felt guilt for such a long time. It wasn't like now, when having a baby that young is almost like having a rosette on your sleeve.

I'd be out and see someone I knew. As I went over

to say hello I could always tell if they were talking about me as I approached. That happened a lot. Some of my friends would chat to me, but behind them I'd see their mothers whispering and poking each other in the ribs about me.

The amazing thing to me was when I returned to Ireland years later for my sister Phyllis's wedding and discovered in conversation with women my age that they'd all been having sex as well, but I didn't know about the places where you could buy condoms on the black market. I wondered why people went on about 'French letters' so much but had no idea. So, for many years I thought it was just me that had had sex, and that by doing so and becoming pregnant, I'd let everybody down.

Eventually one day when Richard was only a few months old, I just couldn't take it anymore. Knowing that he would be well-looked after, since my parents and brothers and sisters doted on him so much, I took it into my head that I had to escape. Although I felt guilty about leaving him, in a strange way I felt that he would be better off if I wasn't on the scene. Then, if I got settled, I would send for him. In many ways it was a childish act, but after the whole business with Seamus and the disapproving glances I received whenever I was out and about, I couldn't think of any other way out. So, packing a few belongings and sneaking out of Wellington Street, I ran away from home, fleeing to, of all places, Barnsley.

My cousin Maureen was living there with her

mother-in-law, but when I turned up she said that she couldn't accommodate me. We looked through the paper and found a barmaid's job. I took it and moved into the pub, writing to my parents and telling them where I was. I stayed there for about six months.

I missed Richard dreadfully and wrote home regularly for news of him. But at the same time I still felt a child myself, and couldn't bear to face the responsibilities that returning would bring. It may seem cruel and heartless, but I was a confused, and, I realise now, immature girl.

Of course my mother wanted me home, and sent my sister Phyllis, who was only fourteen at the time, to bring me back. Phyllis couldn't persuade me – after all she was just a child herself – so she decided to stay as well. I couldn't have her in the pub so had to leave the job. Luckily, there was this chap I was seeing, and his auntie put us up in one of her rooms. Phyllis and I got work in a factory making little medicine bottles. We thought it was great fun, me and Phyllis and all the girls with their hair in turbans and rollers singing together. When I said to Phyllis, 'You'll have to go home,' she refused.

Then we got a telegram: 'Come home. Your father is dangerously ill.'

Like all good Irish girls away from home, I went to the local priest and told him that we had to return to Dublin but didn't have enough money for the boat. For a while he wouldn't have it that I was born and

raised in Ireland but eventually he believed me and
bought us two tickets to go back.

After the crossing, we made our way back to
Wellington Street. As we climbed the stairs to the top
floor I could hear my dad laughing. 'I thought he was
desperately ill,' I said to Phyllis.

So we walked in, and there he was with our mam,
hale and hearty. 'Oh you're back then, are you?' he
boomed.

I quizzed my mother: 'But I thought me da was
ill.'

She just smiled and said, 'I knew that would get
you home.'

I tried to stay in Dublin and make a go of it, but
I just couldn't settle. The embarrassment of walking
down the street with my baby, subjected to the
constant stares, the mutterings, the elbows nudging
each other, became unbearable again.

Please don't get me wrong; I wasn't ashamed of
Richard. There were lots of good people who looked
out for us, like Mrs Carroll in the parlour of
Wellington Street. She was sent parcels from her
family in America and would give me things for
Richard, and my friends were kind, but they were all
at the age where they had jobs and were going out
enjoying themselves. All I was doing was sitting
indoors, brooding on the injustice of Seamus leaving
me with Richard. It wasn't as though it had been a
one-night stand. Seamus and I saw each other for
nearly two years, and so it was hard not to feel hurt

that he had simply walked out of our lives and, so I heard, met somebody else pretty soon afterwards.

In one way I was glad that Seamus wasn't involved in bringing up Richard, because he had proved himself to be a weakling and a coward. But love is strange and contradictory; at the same time as I despised him I also missed him and felt deeply hurt by his rejection of us.

I really needed to get away. After a year or so, when I was nineteen, I persuaded my parents that they should let me go to London and find a job.

'If you get one where you're living in, then OK,' said my mam. 'We have to know that you have a home.' They were more than happy to look after little Richard, but I made the proviso that if and when I met and married somebody, I would send for him. So when I saw an advert in the *Herald* for a job as a live-in barmaid at a pub called the Duchess Of Wellington in Woolwich, south London, I wrote off and got it. One of my brother's friends had been stationed in the army at Woolwich Barracks, and told me that there were loads of soldiers in the area.

'Well I'm not interested in soldiers,' I told him defiantly. I'd been writing to this chap in the Royal Navy and we were getting along fine.

Just after Christmas 1958 I travelled on my own to London via Liverpool. As I came out of the station at Woolwich Arsenal, the Duchess of Wellington loomed on the opposite corner, so there was no chance of getting lost.

The pub was run by a husband and wife. I didn't take to her much. I walked in and introduced myself straight off the boat and minutes later she had me working behind the bar.

Their names are lost to the mists of time, but I remember clearly how bossy she was. In the end I was only there for ten weeks. During that time I wrote to my mam constantly asking after Richard because I missed him so much.

Towards the end of that period, on one of my days off, I told them I was going to buy a dress to send back for my sister Kathy's confirmation.

The landlady asked me to pick up some bits and pieces for her but because the shops were closing early that day, I couldn't get her everything. Now I can't remember exactly what it was, but let's say I failed to pick up a piece of cheese. I had the rashers and the eggs and the bread, but that wasn't good enough.

When I got back, in front of the customers in the pub, she poked me in the shoulder and berated me. 'When I send you on an errand you bring back exactly what I tell you to!' she shouted.

'How dare you?' I said. 'I didn't come here as your errand girl; I came here as a barmaid. This is my day off. I didn't have to get your shopping!'

I was absolutely fuming, goaded on by one of the regulars, an Irishman in his sixties. 'Go on, Dinah, you tell her.'

So, without thinking, I said, 'You can stick your job!'

I don't know what came over me, and almost instantly regretted it, but to my rescue came May O'Dowd, another of the barmaids. As it turned out, May was to play another part in my destiny. And something far greater than saving me my job. She introduced me to her brother. His name was Jeremiah, but he was known as Gerald, Gerry and sometimes Ger. To me he was always Gerald.

My life was never to be the same again.

Chapter Seven

What Have I Done?

Gerald, 1958

He was very handsome.

I remember exactly the first time I set eyes on him: 23 January 1959. It wasn't only my birthday, but his as well. He'd dropped in to the Duchess of Wellington to see his sister May, who did the lunchtime shift when the pub served food. Gerald wasn't too tall, about five feet eight inches, but was broad-shouldered, dark-haired and blue-eyed, with a tailor-made suit, hand-made shirt and shining shoes. He was twenty-four, a real up-to-date type of character. He and his brother David, I was to find out, had their suits made by a tailor called Greenberg in Plumstead Common Road. Very natty.

When May introduced me, I thought, 'Oh he's nice.' We chatted and found out that we shared birthdays, and I served him a pint for free. Thank God the guvnor didn't see that, or there would have been hell to pay.

He started dropping back in to the pub to say hello, and soon asked me out. I told him I couldn't because I was writing to the chap in the navy. The following Saturday I went with May to the Co-op Club in Woolwich and he was there with a girl. He strolled over and said to me casually, 'I won't be long,' left with the girl and came back within a few minutes on his own.

'You shouldn't have done that,' I said, but he explained to me that the woman was just a friend and that they had known each other for years. At the end of the evening he walked me home and we had a bit of a kiss and cuddle. That night I thought about what to do about the bloke in the navy. He knew about Richard and wanted me to wait for him until he came out of the services four years later. But that's an awful long time to expect a young girl to wait, even though in some ways I wish I had now, so I wrote to him and told him it was over.

Before I started with Gerald I told him, 'Look, you'd better know now that I've got a little boy. If ever I meet somebody and marry, I'll have him with me. If you're not interested I understand.' I was nervous, not knowing how he'd react and scared that it would put him off. I wish now it had!

The night I told him he walked away, saying that he needed time on his own to think. A few hours later he came back and said, 'So you've got a baby? So what?' But I was to learn later that other women in his family had illegitimate babies, so maybe it wasn't such a big deal to him. Also I think now that he liked the fact that I'd already had a baby; it showed that I'd had sex and would maybe be more willing than some of the other girls.

It was only a few days after our first date that I told the landlady to stick her job.

On the next shift May asked me what I was going to do. I really didn't know. I didn't have a penny to my name, because what I didn't spend on dressing and feeding myself I sent back to my mam, and now I had no job and no place to stay. I told May of my predicament and she suggested I go with her and ask her mother if I could stay with her family till I got fixed up.

I packed my case and she brought me to her home, 28 Burrage Road, Woolwich. Her mother Maggie was very dark-haired, with that Spanish–Irish look to her, from Tipperary, while her dad, George O'Dowd, was small and none too chatty, from Mote in the west of Ireland, though he'd also spent some time in the north. They all lived together: parents, Gerald, his brother David and the other sisters Pauline and Josephine. May was living back there temporarily, having just divorced.

The house itself was pretty shabby, very badly in

need of repair. The story was that it was supposed to have been demolished after the war, and I believed it. I was very scared, and becoming sorrier by the minute that I had cheeked the landlady of the Duchess of Wellington. What had I done?

May's mother said that I could stay for a while, in the back room downstairs; she obviously recognised how vulnerable I was. I soon learnt that she was the matriarch, and what she said, went. Over the years, no matter how much I tried to please her, I couldn't. Even from the first, she was trying to stir things up. By that time Gerald and I had been out on a couple of dates, and, of course, that first night he was so delighted I was there he tried to sleep in with me. I wasn't having any of it. When Gerald told her we had started seeing each other, she said, 'Well, I know something you don't: she's got a baby.'

'I know that already,' he told her. 'It's nothing to do with you.'

His attitude towards her, and other little actions of his, helped to convince me that he cared and was prepared to accept me for what I was. I was hooked. I have to say that when I fall in love, it is head over heels, and I fell for him very badly. I'm very loyal and don't allow anything to distract from my love for somebody, and maybe that's why I accepted Gerald's behaviour as it became more and more monstrous as the years passed.

I didn't understand at the time that this was all

part of his plausibility, the skilful way he manipulated me throughout our time together. In reality I had walked into the lion's den, but I didn't recognise that for a long time.

I got a new job, shift work from six till two and two till ten at the Tate & Lyle factory across the water from Woolwich. Along with all the other workers I walked down the foot tunnel or got the ferry across there and back, rising at four in the morning to make the first shift.

At that time Gerald was out of work. He told me on our first night out together that he had been an amateur boxer and spent time in the army, extending his national service by three years. He had only come out of the army a year or so before we met. His major vice was fluttering on the gee-gees. There wasn't a day he didn't go to the bookies throughout our life together, more than forty years. It is worth remembering that while reading this book. In hard times and good, Gerald had to gamble, whether it was a couple of bob or a couple of hundred pounds. It was an addiction with him, something which became part of, and had a massive impact on, our lives. As long as he had money it would go to the bookies.

Alcohol had a similarly terrible effect on him during our first year or so. He didn't go on binges, but if Gerald was out having a drink and somebody looked crooked at him, they would get a slap. He had a huge reputation as a fighter in Woolwich. He usually only drank pints, but if he had a whisky he would change and fists would fly. His brother David was a charming man but when he took drink he became a stranger. He'd lost an eye in an accident at school and it had hampered his education; David couldn't read or write and I think his frustrations overcame him when he drank. He felt the stigma because his own family used to laugh at him about it.

Gerald told me that during his time stationed in Wiltshire he had got into a lot of trouble scrapping when drunk. As he told it, he'd also had a regular girlfriend while he was in the army, a local girl; they saw each other for years until one time when he was locked up for some reason. When he came out of the glasshouse he discovered his girl was doing the dirty on him with another bloke. The way he put it was that this was the worst thing that had ever happened to him – he couldn't stand betrayal.

Gerald never seemed to work. He told me on the first night we went out that he had lost his job digging for the Metropolitan Water Board that day. He said he had been sacked unfairly but I later found out he'd been fired for fighting and couldn't claim at the labour exchange because of the way he'd been let go. Anyway, this all seemed immaterial, and soon Gerald and I were going steady. I missed my Richard so much and, as the weeks went by, I fell in love with Gerald. He and I even talked about marriage and I began to see that if I stayed with him I could soon send for Richard. We would be reuinited. It looked like my dreams were coming true.

Indeed our first few weeks at his mother's were happy, but then one night his sister Pauline was playing records in the front room, waiting for her young man to come round and pick her up. I was blissfully unaware of everything in the back room but apparently Gerald stormed in there and insisted on playing his own discs for me to hear. They started rowing and he became so angry that he took his sister's records and smashed them, one by one. His mother came in to calm things down and the upshot was that, even though I hadn't been involved, I had to leave.

'What have I done?' I wailed.

'Just get out,' said his mother. 'Get out of my house and don't come back.'

So, with the little money I was bringing in from Tate & Lyle, I got a room nearby, just off Herbert Road in Plumstead, and Gerald came to live with me.

I said to him, 'You go home to your mother. There's no need for you to live with me like this,' but he refused, sticking up for me. Of course that endeared him to me even more.

But I didn't stay there very long, not more than a couple of weeks. The husband of the house was supposed to be blind, but twice he opened the bedroom door while I was in there, so when I told Gerald I wanted out of there, we moved into a room at his Aunt Kitty's. While we were living at Kitty's, in March 1959, I fell pregnant. Gerald didn't believe in contraception and, never the most affectionate of lovers, was only concerned with getting his way.

Around this time I was writing regularly to my mother so she knew I'd left the pub and had met somebody. I didn't tell her that I was going from pillar to post, or that Gerald's mother had thrown me out of her house. And throughout it all I couldn't even contemplate going back to Dublin. That wasn't an option to me.

I was determined to start my life afresh away from the sneers and the comments, and had resolved never to return to the stifling atmosphere of Wellington Street. Even if it took a bit longer than I first thought to be reunited with Richard, I believed that we would all be happier in the long run if I stuck it out in London. As for the fact that Gerald and I were effectively 'living in sin' neither of us cared a jot. We decided early on that we would marry as soon as the opportunity arose.

But we couldn't stay at his aunt's forever. Gerald got a new job, at the Matchless motorbike factory off Plumstead Common, and we moved again, this time into a room in Burrage Road not far from his mother's. It's funny, but at the time 'living in sin' was considered one of the worst things to do, but his mother didn't seem to have as much of a problem with that as with the fact that I had a baby born out of wedlock back in Ireland.

Nothing seemed to be settled; I was like a nomad. But I think when you're in love, particularly young love, you have this feeling that you can ride any storm and take whatever anybody throws at you, to show the person that you're with how much you love them.

I recognised early on that Gerald was very insecure. Every time he'd lose a job it was never his fault. I'd ask him why he didn't talk to the foreman and ask for some leniency and he'd say, 'You don't understand what they're like. There's no going back there.' So there were periods when he'd have a job, and then it would be the dole, but he'd never have enough stamps from the year before so then he'd be on Social Security. I found that very degrading because he'd send me, cap in hand, to collect it.

By the summer of 1959 I was starting to show so I took to wearing a wedding ring and we told his family. We also decided to marry in November, a month before the baby was due. Gerald was again on Social Security and often in the bookies, sometimes working nights at the pub where his sister worked. By this time I had a job during the day from seven o'clock in the morning till lunchtime, at a cafe in Woolwich which catered to the drivers and clippies from the local bus station. I can remember always running out the back to be sick; the aroma of that fried food turned my stomach in my condition.

Then, one day, while I was serving three fellers, one of them, a cheeky young bus conductor, asked me to go to the pictures with him that afternoon. I flashed the ring, telling him I was married. He held my hand and studied the ring, apologising. I don't know how it happened – maybe divine intervention, or the reverse of it – but at that precise moment Gerald walked past the window. He never walked that way. In fact he should have been across town. I waved to him, thinking he was going to come in, but he didn't. Instead he walked on.

By the time my shift ended I'd forgotten all about the young feller and me showing him my ring. It had all been totally innocent anyway so what was to dwell on?

I walked home to Burrage Road and no sooner had I opened the door to our room than, whack! I was punched full in the face and sent reeling across the room to the floor.

He came at me and I screamed, 'Stop, stop, stop! What's wrong? What have I done? Please tell me what I've done wrong.'

'I saw that geezer in the cafe!' Gerald raged, purple-faced. 'I saw him holding your hand!'

As I cowered, holding my hands around my stomach to protect our unborn child, I groaned, 'I was just showing him my wedding ring, Gerald. He asked me out and I said I couldn't go because I'm with you. Please believe me. The chap did nothing wrong, and neither did I.'

It took a full five minutes, with me shaking with fear, for him to calm down. All of that time he ranted and raved that I had gone behind his back, flirting and deliberately coming on to the bloke in the cafe. It was crystal clear from what I was saying that I wasn't lying and eventually he got down on the floor with me.

I cried, 'I've got a pain in my stomach, Gerald. What's going on?'

Then came the inevitable apologies and excuses. He kissed me, saying again and again that he was sorry. 'I'll get the doctor; everything will be all right,' he said.

I don't know what he told the doctor, but when he arrived I saw in his eyes that he knew even though I didn't have any marks to my face right away. The bruising didn't come out until later. The doctor examined me and said, 'I think everything will be all right, but if this pain continues come and see me at the surgery.'

When the doctor had gone, Gerald and I talked. He made me cups of tea and offered to take me to see his Aunt Kitty, because he knew I liked her. He also kept on saying over and over that, above all else, he hated betrayal because he had been so cruelly cheated by that girl when he was in the army, and the thought of me going behind his back had set him off.

I assured him I would never do that but as I spoke at the back of my mind huge doubts were nagging. Nobody in my life had treated me like that. Sure my mam and dad had slapped me and used the strap on me if I was naughty but this was different. His temper was one thing, but here I was stuck with a man prepared to hit a pregnant woman. What could I do? Where could I go? I couldn't return home again, not with another baby. What would that do to my poor parents?

I was so frightened by the experience. It shook me to the core. Without my family around me I decided to take drastic action. In my stupidity, the very next day when Gerald was out at work, I asked a friend about getting rid of my baby. That way, my twisted thinking ran, I could escape his clutches. Suddenly Dublin seemed at least a refuge from the kind of punishment Gerald revealed himself capable of meting out.

My friend told me about these crystals called Isinglass. I went straight to the chemist and bought myself a packet.

Hurriedly I rushed back to Burrage Road and ran a very hot bath. I sprinkled the Isinglass into it, and gingerly eased myself into the steaming water. It was absolute agony, and, of course, absolutely ineffective.

I ended up looking like a scalded lobster and made myself very ill. I called the doctor again. He asked me why I had done it. I told him I couldn't face having the baby but never told him about Gerald's treatment of me.

I tried to console myself with the hope that Gerald's attack had been a one-off. Of course it wasn't. Instead it was the start, the point at which my life slid downhill.

Gerald's Social Security didn't go very far, but whenever I wrote home to my family, I kept everything light, not mentioning our hardship. Gerald swore it would never happen again and I forced myself to believe him. Here I was, just nineteen, already with one baby whose father had rejected me. I believed Gerald did genuinely love me, and of course I loved him. You may think I was a blind romantic, but I really thought that love would help me conquer all.

Despite the fact that Gerald's ugly side was now coming to the fore, I still couldn't resist him. He seemed so strong and handsome and could often be charming and lovely. I still felt very secure with him, which may sound odd but is the kind of contradiction typical to many abusive relationships.

But Gerald held grudges, and one in particular dated back to a fight he'd had with a few fellers years before I'd met him. During that scrap he'd had a piece of one of his ears bitten off. One night, when I was eight months pregnant, he left the pub in a hell of a state looking for the geezer that had chewed his ear. Like a lunatic I was chasing after him, but he wouldn't listen, going from the Co-op Club to the Catholic Club searching in vain.

Eventually he came home but was obviously still simmering, because the very next night, at his cousin Jimmy's wedding reception, in the big room above the Queen's Arms in Burrage Road, he knocked another feller out for no reason at all.

During the evening Jimmy had been having some playful fun with a friend of his, though it looked to Gerald as though this bloke had given him a shove. He put two and two together and got five, walked over and said, 'Are you arguing with my cousin?' Before he could answer Gerald punched him full in the face, knocking him sparko.

We spent that night at his mother's house across

the road, along with several other people, including the bloke he'd punched. The next morning Gerald saw his black eye and said, 'Oh my God, what happened to you?'

'Are you taking the mick? Don't you remember? You did that,' said the guy.

When I confirmed it, Gerald was distraught, and vowed to give up drinking. It was one promise which by and large he kept.

Times were very tough, but I was delighted when we married on 28 November 1959 at St Peter's Church in Woolwich. There was just us and his sister May and her boyfriend. We didn't even have a photograph taken, and Gerald's parents and the rest of his family made a point of not turning up. It was all over so quickly but, after all, I was pregnant so it wasn't going to be a big do. I wore a lilac coat and full skirts and petticoats which helped disguise my bump. I have to say I was still really pleased to wear the twelve-pound ring he had bought me.

That day was the first time I encountered what we called a queer or a poof in those days. I'd heard people refer to 'powder puffs' in Ireland but didn't know what it meant, even though I had worked with a chap who was very feminine and used to mince around a lot.

As we sat in the pub after the wedding service sipping our drinks I spotted this great big chap at the bar. 'That man's got nail varnish on,' I whispered to Gerald. 'And mascara! And lipstick!'

Gerald turned to me and said, 'He's queer, Dinah! Don't you know what one of those is?'

Apparently this man worked as an usher in the local cinema. I was totally green about homosexuals; little did I know I was going to have one myself in a couple of years time!

We had our drink in the pub and a pie, and I was happy. The fact that this time there would be no shame attached to the birth of my child made a big difference to me; I felt as though Gerald had made an honest woman of me.

When we visited his parents later that day, Maggie O'Dowd wasn't exactly effusive. 'Well it's all over now,' she said. 'You're married and that's it.'

Within a few weeks there was another upheaval. We had to leave the room in Burrage Road as the landlady's son was coming back home and needed it.

So we moved to a place further up in Plumstead, Wickham Lane. The old boy who owned it was a peculiar little feller. He was forever telling us how strong he was, and how one day he'd got hold of this bloke who lived there and held him over his head before throwing him down the stairs. I don't know whether he was a bit frightened of Gerald because of his size, but he kept on going on about it.

One day when Gerald was out I decided to move the room around. I was heavily pregnant by then and must have made a hell of a noise shifting the furniture about because when Gerald got home the old boy complained to him: 'She's had somebody up there today.' He flew up the stairs and confronted me. I told him that nobody had been around, because that was the truth; there was just me rearranging the room. I was always doing that.

I'd done it since I was a kid. My father would come home and say, 'Where's the bed?' because I'd moved it behind the door. It's funny because all my sisters did the same thing. If any of us had a new vase, say, then we'd change the furniture around to accommodate it.

Anyway, back at Wickham Lane, Gerald went down and told the old boy that all he had heard was the sound of me on my own shifting furniture. 'There's no way that little girl can have moved that wardrobe on her own!' the old man protested. For once Gerald was in my corner: 'No, no, no, it's just a thing she does; don't worry about it.' But this funny feller would have none of it, and soon the rent started creeping up and we couldn't afford to live there. So once again, for the sixth time that fateful year, I was on the move. We took rooms in Herbert Road, again in Plumstead, and that's where we lived when Kevin was born.

Chapter Eight

Why is He Doing This to Me?

With my hair dyed black, in a two-tiered skirt I bought from Martin Ford's, 1960

I was awestruck when I first set eyes on Kevin. He was absolutely beautiful-looking; I've never seen a baby so pretty, with masses of black hair. He was big enough, at seven pounds ten ounces. The nurse who took me along said, 'Wait till you see him. I've fallen in love with him meself.' She'd brushed his hair in a marcel wave and it looked lovely. I said, 'That's not my baby,' and she said, 'Yes, it is!'

I had been put down for a Christmas baby, having suffered pains around the 23rd. The nurse told me that if I didn't give birth by the 25th, they would induce me. As it turned out another woman came in and had hers on Christmas Day, so Kevin took a bit longer and came into this world on 29 December 1959.

Kevin's birth also brought out my maternal instincts towards Richard. I had kept in contact with my mam, who was updating me by weekly letter on his progress. It was awful not seeing him grow up at first hand but I received photographs which gave me some solace. However, as I held Kevin in my arms I howled, crying over having left Richard behind. I felt awful pangs of guilt. I knew I loved Richard from the moment I had him but now I wondered whether I should have brought him with me. I also vowed to myself that he would come to me as soon as possible. Even if Gerald walked away from me after Kevin was born, I was determined that Richard would join his new little brother in London.

I had no idea for a name for our baby. Gerald begged me to call him Kevin, after the twin of his brother David, who hadn't survived a fall his mother suffered when she was pregnant. His full name is Anthony Kevin, but I didn't want anybody shortening it to Tony, so he became our little Kevin.

Gerald's brother David was over the moon, cock-a-hoop. He showed more enthusiasm for the baby than the father. I was the only mother who didn't have any flowers, but I consoled myself by thinking that Gerald was shy and didn't know how to express his feelings. I did ask him why he hadn't bought any and he exclaimed, 'I couldn't carry them down the street with everyone looking at me.' He never was one for public signs of affection. I could never hold his hand or put my arm through his. I'd ask him why not, because I wanted everybody to know we were together in love, but he'd tell me I was just being silly.

In fact he hardly showed any signs of affection anywhere. 'Why can't you tell me, "I love you,"?' I'd ask him, but he would just grimace and shake his head. The only time he said it was when we were in bed. If there was anything romantic or sentimental on the television he'd just groan, 'Oh God, look at all this crap,' so, in the beginning at least, I decided to put it down to shyness.

I found him very hard to please, because I was so open in showing my emotions, and he was so closed. It's difficult even now, all these years later, to put into words the effect it had on me. I'd wonder to myself: 'Does he really care about me? Does he love me?' But he was the most perplexing man. He'd do something, buy something nice for the house, which would make me think he did love me after all. He'd ask, shyly, 'Do you like it?' and be really pleased when I said how nice it was. But then he would constantly hint about how much it cost. As the days went by he'd say, 'Now take care of that. It cost a lot of money, you know.'

I remember once he bought me a ring. I told him, 'Now I don't want to know how much it was. I don't care if it cost sixpence. You bought it for me and that's the main thing. You thought about it, and that's really nice.' That's the way I am. Even if I didn't like a present, I'd never say so. But he couldn't help himself and he had to let me know the price. That was just one of the aspects of his character which bemused me.

For a while now he hadn't shown any more tendencies to violence beyond hollering and shouting. By this time we had moved to rooms in Wrottesley Road, off Plumstead Common, and Gerald was working as a painter and decorator for a company run by the brother of our GP, Dr Lockett. But it wasn't long before rows started to develop at Wrottesley Road because the landlady kept on putting the rent up. We went to the tribunal and they ruled in our favour, what little good it did us. She had claimed that I was dirty and slovenly but the inspectors came and checked out the kitchen and the rooms and gave us a clean bill.

What was ironic, given there was so much prejudice at the time, when a regular notice in the windows of houses with rooms to let read: 'No Irish, no blacks, no dogs' – was that the landlady was black herself, a Jamaican. She was obviously sore about having lost, and one night there was a massive row. The tenants upstairs, who were also black, were banging on the floor and the landlady was shouting that she wanted us out. The police were called when Gerald got into a fight with one of the blokes upstairs. It seemed to calm down, but the very next day another argument kicked off, and Gerald hit the bloke upstairs and knocked him out. Again the police were called and needless to say our days there were numbered.

In order to afford new rooms I took a job doing shifts at a factory in Abbey Wood, again from six o'clock in the morning till two in the afternoon, and then two till ten at night. The job was so mundane I can't even remember what the factory produced, but I thought that, with us both working, we'd be better off. Gerald's Aunt Kitty said she'd look after Kevin for me while I was at work.

Gerald now had a job doing nights at a factory, and one particular morning he got home and went to bed. Around lunchtime I made him his tea and gave him his newspaper before going off to work myself. 'Can you get me my tobacco?' he asked as I was getting ready. So I did that and was just about to leave when he asked me for something else. 'Gerald!' I said sharply. 'You're gonna make me late for work as it is. Do it yourself!'

He started swearing at me and I remember saying, 'Kiss my arse!' and slammed the door behind me in my rush to get the bus to work. You see, even though he had already started on his campaign of abuse, there was still something of the spirited girl in me, and I saw no reason why I should not answer him back, in just the same way that I would cheek my elder brothers or anyone else in my life. Of course that was all to change, but for the time being I slammed the door behind me in my rush to catch my bus, and off I went to work. That night I caught the same bus home and there he was, waiting for me at my stop.

'Oh hello, darling,' I said innocently, but suddenly, smack! He punched me right in the face. There were plenty of people around getting off the bus or waiting at the stop, and everyone jumped back. There was a hush.

I shrieked, 'What's the matter? What's the matter?!' and he grabbed me by the hair and dragged me towards Kitty's, punching and kicking me, shouting, 'You fucking bitch! You never talk to me like that!'

At first I struggled and cried out but he would have none of it, and just ignored me. So a pattern was set. I knew that screaming would do me no good so learnt to take what he doled out to me.

Of course it was only the women who remonstrated: 'That's disgusting! Leave the poor girl alone!' He told them to stick it and punched and dragged me by the hair all the way to Kitty's, about half a mile.

When we got there he didn't let up, even though there was another relative of his, Violet Hayes, present. When they tried to reason with him he told them that it was none of their business, that they should keep out of it as well. Although Kitty and Violet pleaded and pleaded with him he just went on and on until he was spent. I was so badly beaten I had bruises everywhere and couldn't go to work for two and a half weeks. My face looked like I'd done several rounds with Cassius Clay.

I stayed in, refusing to go out. 'I'll get yer shopping for you,' he'd say.

'You'll have to,' I told him. 'I can't go out looking like this.'

Eventually I plucked up the courage and nipped down to the local shop for a paper and some cigarettes. 'Oh my God, what's happened to you?' said the woman behind the counter.

'Oh, me husband hit me,' I said nonchalantly. I was so wild that he had punched me and given me that black eye. Before, all the bruises and injuries had been on my body, arms and legs, and could be covered up.

'No! I don't believe you!' she said.

'OK then, he didn't hit me,' I snapped, paid her and went home.

When Gerald got back he was full of questions: 'Who got you those fags? Where did you get that paper?'

'I went down the shops, Gerald,' I announced.

'Did anyone say anything to you?' he asked.

'Yes. The lady in the shop asked about my black eye and I told her you gave it to me.' It may sound strange, but I wasn't scared to speak my mind, even though it might have invited another beating. That's an Irish trait, not backing down. And you see by that time I'd had a few hidings and was learning to ride the punches.

I saw that he was shocked by the fact that somebody else knew what he was like. I'd spotted a weakness of his: he actually cared what other people thought of him and never wanted the truth of his violent nature to be revealed. I was learning to understand how his mind worked.

He said, 'Oh that's nice, innit? What's she gonna think of me now? I said I was sorry, didn't I?'

Eventually we had to leave Wrottesley Road because of all the trouble with the landlady. Gerald asked his mother if we could stay with her, but she turned him down, so that first night we slept on Woolwich Common. Kevin was well wrapped up in his pram but I was already a few months gone with Georgie. I remember crying to myself all night. I'd had to leave all my belongings behind for us to pick up when we got new digs. 'I can't believe this is happening,' I kept on saying to myself. He was apologetic, but I told him it wasn't his fault.

The next day Gerald went to his mother again and she relented, so we moved into a single room back in Burrage Road. But it was the worst place to be. There was never any peace; instead, there was absolute turmoil, with all of them – his mam and dad, May and Pauline – at each other's throats twenty-four hours a day, shouting and arguing all the while. They would row over the stupidest things. One of them would put a pan of water on and then another would come in and take it off the heat and all hell would break loose. Never in my life had I heard a family row so much. And this was the atmosphere Gerald had been brought up in.

Kevin was such a tiny little thing and I feared that his nerves would be shot. Even today I wonder what effect that environment of forty years ago had on his life. Our room was eight by ten feet, enough room for Kevin's cot and a single bed in which we both slept. And although he wasn't too tall, Gerald was a big feller, about fifteen stone at the time. One day Kevin took ill. A few days earlier we'd had pork chops which I'd mashed up with a little bit of potato for him, and there was obviously a delayed reaction because suddenly he started to throw up. I was given some medicine so we tried that but it didn't seem to help. Within twenty-four hours he seemed to be wasting away, just these massive big eyes but no flesh on him. I was petrified.

I sent for Dr Lockett. He couldn't diagnose what was causing the problem and said, 'This child is seriously ill and has to go to hospital.' We rushed Kevin into Hither Green Hospital and he was soon surrounded by doctors and nurses.

They asked me to wait outside and then one came to see me and said gravely, 'I'm afraid he's going to have to have the last rites.' At that, my world fell apart. I was terrified that I was going to lose him. But then his fortunes turned and he started to fight back and in the event made a miraculous recovery. By ten o'clock that night he had made such progress, it was decided that it would be best all round if Gerald and I went home, got some sleep and returned in the morning.

When we got off the bus there had been a power cut on Plumstead Common. Gerald said he was going to do his usual stint in his sister's pub, the Sussex Arms, and I asked whether I could go with him because I didn't want to be on my own worrying about Kevin, particularly in the dark.

'Yes, of course you can,' he said, in that way he had when he seemed to be so understanding. So while he was behind the bar I sat in the snug and waited. Then, about ten minutes later, two young chaps came into the main bar, and Gerald served them. Within seconds he appeared in the snug and snapped at me, 'Get home.'

I was confused. 'Why? Can't I stay?'

For some reason, he was furious. 'I told you! Get the fuck out of here and go home!'

I tried to reason with him: 'But there's nobody there. Your mam's going to be coming round here soon and I don't want to be on my own tonight.'

But he would have none of it: 'I don't care – get out!' So I left.

On the way back I met his mam and two sisters and told them what had happened to Kevin and also that I'd been ordered out of the pub. I asked them to find out what I had done wrong. 'He's made me come home,' I cried. 'I haven't done anything. I was sitting there and two fellers came in and the next thing I knew he told me to get out. I haven't done anything.'

What hadn't occurred to me was that the Sussex Arms at that time had mirrors everywhere, all over the walls, so you could see everyone who was in there from any position. Obviously those two blokes had spied me sitting in the snug and said something about me in front of Gerald.

When I got back to the tiny room I was feeling very down. It all seemed so unfair. Earlier on in the evening Gerald had been nice as pie, taking me to the pub because of the power cut. Then, for no reason, he virtually pushed me out into the dark night. He knew how upset I was about Kevin and I certainly hadn't done anything to provoke those guys, so why was I being punished? I made a bed up on the floor, putting a little mattress in front of Kevin's cot. I heard the family come back, but Gerald wasn't among them, because he usually had to stay late to help clean the pub up.

I was lying in the dark when he finally came home.

'What's that?' Gerald demanded, towering over me in the little bed.

I told him very calmly, 'I'm sleeping here tonight.'

'Are you? Why?' he shouted.

'Because I want to,' I said standing up, and, with that, he went for me, trying to grab at me.

I whimpered, 'Don't touch me, don't touch me. The baby. Please don't hurt me.' But it was no good. He punched me, kicked me – like a wild animal, he was. I went down onto the floor and my first thought was to curl up into a ball, thinking to myself, 'Surely he won't hurt the baby.' I was screaming and screaming and you know what? In that full house –

with all of them in the front room – nobody, not one of them, came to my aid for the longest time as he lashed into me.

His sister May did eventually shout through the door, 'Gerald, will you stop it?' But he just screamed back, 'Keep out of this; it's got nothing to do with you.' So that was it, off she went.

Then, finally, his dad burst in and went absolutely bonkers. He was only a tiny little man, but he picked a hefty bowl up and shouted at Gerald, 'You punch that girl once more and I'll whack this over your head.'

At first Gerald would have none of that. 'This is none of your business,' he yelled.

'It is my business, because this is *my* house,' said his dad. 'I will not have anybody treating people like this here!'

The fact that his old man had gone berserk seemed to get through to Gerald: he suddenly stopped hitting me and strode out of the house. There was an eerie silence and his dad left the room. I lay on the floor as pain seemed to penetrate every part of my body. I could hear them all going to their bedrooms.

In the darkness I crawled along the passage and went into his mam's room at the front of the house. 'Can somebody help me?' I wailed. 'Why is he doing this to me?'

She said coldly, 'I've told you before not to answer him back, and you keep doing it. You should know by now. You know what a terrible temper he has.'

I told her I wasn't his slave and had a right to say what I wanted.

She said, 'You of all people should understand it's best not to say anything at all.'

So I slunk to bed, the pain in my tummy so intense, sobbing at the torment. With Kevin in hospital and God knows what pain or injuries had been caused to my baby, I had never felt more alone.

And then, hours later – as part of the pattern which was to become so familiar – there he was, back in the room and full of remorse. With tears streaming down his face he begged forgiveness. 'I don't know what happened to me. I'm sorry, I'm sorry. I promise, I promise it'll never happen again. I'll go to church, confess and swear to God I'll never do it again.'

I told him that I was too exhausted to talk but that we couldn't continue living like this. After a while we settled down, but I couldn't sleep. I was beginning to seriously worry about the baby; the pains were severe, but the worst thing was dealing with the fear. It may sound strange but in those circumstances terror is the most painful thing, almost physical.

It wasn't so much being scared of him or worrying that he might do it again, but more the disbelief that he had done what he had done while I was pregnant. I was having his baby – how could he do this to us?

But at the same time I had two children with another on the way, so where could I go? I couldn't go home to my mam. If I had told her that he was beating the hell out of me, she would have taken me in, I knew that, but I couldn't tell her the truth. I was too proud and too ashamed.

I had made a mistake before – over Seamus – and couldn't admit that I had made a mistake again. And even though Gerald was the one who was administering the beatings, I felt it was my fault. I honestly believed that I must have done something wrong to deserve it.

I hadn't listened to his mother's advice about not answering him back so I thought I was the one to blame. That's what manipulative, abusive people do: they make their victims feel they are the guilty parties. It's unbelievable to me now, looking back on it at this distance and with all my experience, but that is truly how I felt.

It also echoed my childhood; when I was being walloped by Gerald for answering back I remembered how that would happen as a kid, that I'd feel the back of the old man's hand if I got cheeky. So, weirdly, I said to myself, 'Maybe I deserve this.'

When Gerald would control me, say, by questioning my every move – 'You said you were only going to be five minutes when you went to the shops but you've been twenty. What do you think is going through my head?' – he was convincing me that I was in the wrong. It was subtle but very effective.

After the beatings, after the heartfelt apologies, after the swearing to God it would never happen again, I would find myself saying to him, 'I'll make it up to you. I'll never give you cause to hit me again.'

I also learnt not to say too much. At first, when I came home from a day's work, I'd be like any normal person, open and honest, telling him about what had happened: 'Oh we had a laugh today, this feller Johnny came in and was so funny.' But he'd store it all away. Two weeks down the line during an argument he'd say, 'Oh was Johnny being funny again? Don't you remember telling me about Johnny?'

Everything joyful seemed to be sullied. He'd put a nasty edge on any experience I had, so I resolved to censor what I said about other people, particularly men. But eventually even that turned in on me. 'Well? What happened today?' he'd demand.

'Nothing really,' I'd mutter.

'What? You were at work all day and nothing happened? I don't believe you!'

You couldn't win either way.

It was his ability to manipulate me which had got me in such a state after the incident with the fellers in the Sussex Arms. Maybe I *had* looked at them, causing them to make some comment about me, I thought.

Eventually, Gerald told me what had happened. After ordering their drinks from him, the two blokes had seen me in the mirror and said to him, 'Who's that bit of crumpet?'

Instead of saying, 'Well actually that bit of crumpet is my wife, so watch your tongue,' he chose to brood on it and turned on me. And the way he told me the story only underlined my feelings that maybe I had

attracted their attention. It was my fault again. Then
Gerald piled it on, once again talking about the girlfriend who had done the dirty on him when he was
in the army, and how that experience had scarred
him for life. But I look back now and think I bet
she did no such thing. She was more likely driven
away by his jealous rages; I bet she spoke to somebody once and he took it the wrong way. It was all
a convenient fantasy to make him more sympathetic
to me.

Nevertheless, having heard the tale of the two
blokes calling me 'a bit of crumpet', I promised him
that I wouldn't attract attention in that way again.
So I became withdrawn. I had no friends or family,
only him, and learned not to answer back, covering
my hair with a scarf, not wearing any make-up and
avoiding all but the dowdiest clothes. He'd say, if I
was a bit dolled-up of an evening, 'You can take that
off; you're not going out dressed like that. That
doesn't suit you at all. Take it off.' And I would,
replacing it with something frumpy, so that nobody
would look at me. If anybody paid me any attention
I knew I would get it from him later.

I've asked myself many times where Gerald's
psychosis – and I believe it was that – sprang from.
It certainly wasn't his dad. Fathers can become role
models in these situations, but his was a small man,
usually pretty timid – anything for a quiet life. There
were many things Gerald himself blamed his temper
on, but it's obvious to me that the discipline of his

army years suited his temperament. The problem was that when he came out he was like a loose cannon.

As the years went by I learnt to be ten yards ahead of him; I knew what he was going to say and what he was going to do, and in that way I knew how to protect myself and survive.

Chapter Nine

You've Made Your Bed, Now You Must Lie in It

In Joan Crescent, 1968

As it turned out, I had also learnt to protect my unborn children during the beatings; Georgie was born on 14 June 1961 at Barnhurst and Bexleyheath Hospital, blonde, blue-eyed and bonny as could be. It seemed, by then, I had developed a way of absorbing the injuries without my babies being affected.

When Georgie was ten months old my mam wrote and asked me to go back to Dublin for my sister Phyllis's wedding. By this time my parents were living in Birmingham. Dad had been working there but became ill because of his weak lungs so my mam went to join him and stayed, mainly because she was so sick on the ferry over. When she arrived she said to him, 'I'm not going back Frank, I can't face it,' so she looked after him and got a job as a live-in housemaid.

After the wedding the oldest ones, Annie, Frank, John and Phyllis, were sending the younger girls, Marie, Kathy and Teresa, to join Mam and Dad. Teresa was to be flown over; she was in hospital because of her condition. In a way Phyllis's wedding was going to be the last of Wellington Street, and I didn't want to miss that for the world.

Gerald had a job during the day at a local factory and still did nights at the Sussex Arms, so I asked if it was OK if I took the boys back on my own. It was like that: I had to seek his permission; I couldn't do anything without asking him first. He controlled every aspect of my life and I was too scared to defy him.

He said that I could go, but just before I left for the ferry with Kevin and Georgie, Gerald took me to one side. 'Now you promise me you will come back,' he said. 'Of course I will,' I responded. He repeated his demand: 'Promise me. You have to promise me.' That's how insecure he was. His parting words, even after he had put us on the train at Paddington, were almost a plea: 'You're definitely coming back, aren't you?' I told him, 'If I make a promise I don't break it.'

When I arrived in Dublin, my family were shocked at the sight of me, stunned at how thin I was. I had no breasts and had hollows in my cheeks and neck, the toll taken by the anxiety and fear I experienced during life with Gerald. I knew full well how my looks had deteriorated, but when they questioned me about it, I assured them everything was fine.

I had a lovely time being back home, and was so proud of my little boys. George kept on going on about 'Da Da Da', as babies do, and when Kevin, who was just over two years old, met Richard, who was five, for the first time he walked straight over to his half-brother and, without saying a word, put his arms around him and gave Richard a great big hug. It was heartbreaking to watch not just because of Kevin's sweet gesture, but also because I knew I would have to leave Richard behind again because we had no room for him back in London.

Anyway, there was great happiness on that trip, and when I got back home Gerald was full of enthusiasm. 'I have a surprise for you,' he said, handing me an envelope from the council. 'Open it,' he said excitedly.

An application we had made to the council for a new home had come through. 'Dear Mr and Mrs O'Dowd,' it read. 'We are pleased to offer you a residence, a three-bedroom house at 29 Joan Crescent, Eltham.' I was absolutely over the moon, and not just because we were finally leaving rooms behind. I thought that if Gerald had his own house he would be totally different, that no longer living in cramped spaces on other people's property would have a positive effect on him.

Immediately I received the news I set in motion

plans for Richard to come and join us. He and I had been separated for too long, and although he was slightly older than the other boys and showed signs of his Dublin upbringing, his lovely caring nature meant that he fitted right in with us. To his credit, Gerald always showed him as much love and affection as he did our other kids. All the while Gerald took his violence out on me, he would never do it in front of the children, but when they were out or in bed. And it was great for a while.

When we moved in to that house I had nothing beyond the cot some lady had given me, and a double bed with hefty springs poking through. I didn't even have a spoon, so Gerald's mother gave us a couple of them and a few towels. I hired a cooker off the gas company, we got a grant for bedding and towels and crockery, and I scoured jumble sales, adapting and mending clothes for the kids with an ancient sewing machine. I do know quality fabrics so I'd hunt them down; if I came across a massive pair of decent men's trousers in dogtooth check, I'd get two pairs out of them for my two little ones, and I'd undo hand-made jumpers, steam the wool and make a couple of new ones. I would only pay tuppence but the boys would have beautiful new jumpers.

A lady two doors down from me showed me how to crochet and I added that to the skills that my mam gave me: knitting, sewing, darning. I started to make curtains and quilt covers, usually in nylon, which was fashionable at the time. You'd slip off the bed with those, but they were great for when the children wet the bed because they were washed and ironed in minutes!

The Social helped us to furnish the house. It was all second-hand stuff but I didn't care. The fact that I could shut my front door and there wouldn't be anybody coming in unless I invited them was fantastic. My kids had space and a back garden to play in, and the fact I was finally able to bring Richard over from Dublin made me full of the joys of spring. Gerald didn't have a problem with Richard arriving. To us it was a big house; when we first went round there, Kevin jumped into a cupboard in the front room and said, 'Look, Mummy, here's another bedroom!' Bless him, he was only a little titch, but after what we had been used to, this was a mansion.

For a while there, Gerald stayed on the dole and then he started to get itchy, setting up in business with his brother-in-law doing photography for weddings and the like, but even that didn't satisfy him.

He built a chicken run in the garden, which didn't please others in the Crescent, and dug up the flower beds to grow potatoes, but was always restless, always going on about becoming a boxer. I'd say to him, 'If you think you're that good, why don't you give it a go? You're still young enough. I'll come down to the gym with you and give you all my support.'

'Nah, nah, I can't be bothered,' he'd mutter, but

then he'd start again, saying that he was better than most boxers around. It was an obsession with him, but one he would never do anything about, as if he was afraid of failing. I began to realise that the man I had married was not only very violent but complex and strange as well. To look at him you'd never think it, but he was deeply insecure. Maybe that's why aggression was part of his day-to-day manner. He'd boast to the kids about how many blokes he'd knocked out at some dance hall. I'd plead with him: 'Don't be going on like that to them, they're only little babies,' but he'd tell me to shut up and continue regaling them. 'They've got to be tough,' he'd exclaim, and of course they were mesmerised, thinking that their father was fantastic.

They would tell other kids in the street and he started to get a reputation, which I found pathetic. There was very little violence in my background. OK, we argued and my father would whack my brothers if they got out of line, but this was something different.

Even though he now had the photography business, we were still really hard up. Don't ask me where the money he earned went – I wasn't allowed to enquire – but I had come to know the depth of his gambling addiction during our time at Burrage Road. There'd be five or ten shillings wasted on every race. It doesn't sound a lot but it made a difference to our lives, and, of course, as he got more money the higher the stakes became.

So, by 1962, I had Richard, Kevin and George with me, though I had also lost two babies, one in Burrage Road and one in Joan Crescent. When I had my second miscarriage I remember thinking, 'I'm being punished now for what I'd tried to do with Kevin; I can't have any more children.'

A girl moved in next door at number 27, Heather Higgins, and she was to become a great friend. She'd say to me, 'Don't be silly now, it's not your fault.'

What struck me about Heather was her relationship with her husband. Jimmy would do anything for her around the house, taking the kids out and playing with them; he was everything a father should be. Jimmy ran a football club, which Kevin and Richard joined. He took them all on trips away, even to Holland. Our kids called the Higgins's children Denise, Jimmy and Sean their cousins, we were that close.

When Gerald acted up, Heather would say to me, 'My Jimmy would never do that.' Jimmy and I would sometimes argue, but only in discussions over various subjects, not in an aggressive way. Heather would say, 'Jimmy, will you leave the girl alone?' and he'd respond, 'No, she likes it,' and it was true; I enjoyed having a decent conversation and an exchange of views without it descending into pig ignorance and aggression. What surprised me was that Gerald was fine about it, even though he didn't trust Jimmy. But then he didn't trust anybody.

We never seemed to see any money from the

photography business. One particular Saturday afternoon I'd just put our tea on the table when Gerald demanded the remaining ten pounds I had for housekeeping, saying that he needed to buy some photographic supplies.

'Why has it always got to be you that buys this stuff?' I asked. 'Why not your brother-in-law?'

He started yelling at me and I thought, 'I can't stick this anymore.' So I took the tenner out of my purse and handed it over. 'Now,' I said, 'we have no money till I collect my giro in five days' time. When the kids are hungry and asking for food, you tell them where the money went. When the gas meter runs out and when we haven't got anything to light the fire, you tell them why.'

His ranting and raving went into overdrive. He banged and slammed in and out of the room, raging and shouting at me, working himself up into a lather. He picked up his plate and smashed it against the wall, and then threw a vase after it.

By this time little Kevin was cowering under the table. Gerald took the ten-pound note and threw it onto the coal fire, but my little Richard, who had also been watching, scurried across and rescued it from the flames. Gerald didn't even notice, he was that apoplectic. 'I tell you what,' he yelled. 'You take your kids and stick 'em up your arse and leave 'em there, because I'm fucking sick of them and you!' With that, off he went, slamming out of the house.

I stood there sobbing. I didn't have a plan, or even

a thought in my head. As though I was on autopilot I placed Georgie in the pushchair, put coats on Richard and Kevin, and taking the money, left the house. I don't remember whether I was wearing a coat myself; I certainly didn't pack a bag. I just wanted to go.

We walked all the way down to Mottingham station and caught a train to Euston and then another to Birmingham. On that train I fell to pieces, just sat there crying as the boys looked on, so upset to see their mam in such a state.

The ticket collector asked me if I was all right. 'No, I'm not,' I sobbed. 'I don't know what I've done. I've left home and have to get to my mam's. I've no food for the kids, nothing.'

That kind man gave Richard half a crown and said to him, 'You go and get your brothers and your mum some sandwiches and some tea.' When Richard toddled off, he said, 'I won't let anyone else in this carriage. You stay here and take care of yourself.'

When I asked for his address so that I could repay him, he said, 'Don't worry. Maybe some day along the way we'll meet and you can give it back to me.' That was the kindest gesture I received during that period of my life.

Eventually we arrived at my mother's in Ladypool. She was looking after this old boy who had lost his wife, and the local nuns had asked her to be his housekeeper. She lived in the house with my dad and my sisters Kathy and Marie. There was barely enough room for all of them, let alone me and my three little ones.

We turned up in torrential rain, like drowned rats. When I knocked at the house my sister opened the door and said, 'We don't want no pegs – go 'way!' and slammed the door in my face, thinking we were tinkers.

Soaked through, I hammered on the door, shouting, 'Kitty, Kitty, it's me!'

She opened up again, looked me over and cried, 'Oh quick, Mam. Mam, Mam, it's Dinah . . .'

My mother flew to the door and I blurted out, 'I've left him. I've left him!'

She got us all inside and tried to calm me. She dried me and fetched me dry clothes belonging to one of my sisters. We then warmed the kids and got them a drink.

'Where's their clothes?' Mam asked.

'I didn't bring anything with me,' I confessed. 'I just ran. He was ranting and raving and I didn't want to be hurt again.'

'What do you mean?'

'He's hit me before, Mam,' I said. This was the first time I'd admitted it to my parents.

'Bastard,' she said. 'I'll kill him.'

But as my mother raged, my dad sat me down and said quietly, 'Now listen, chicken. You can't take the children away from their father.'

'I don't want to go back, Dad,' I said. 'I'm not going!'

He became angry, seemingly for no reason. He was the person I thought would stick up for me most in the world, but he didn't. Instead he said, 'I'm sorry, love, but they are his children and he has got a right.'

When I tried to argue with him he just said, 'You've made your bed, now you must lie in it.'

I'll never forget that, nor the words my mother said to me later: 'You'll cry salty tears, my girl. I never liked him the first time I clapped eyes on him.'

She wanted me to stay, but I understood my father. He was of the era of that John Wayne film *The Quiet Man*, you know? 'Here's a stick to beat the lovely lady with.'

My mother said, 'She doesn't have to go back if she doesn't want to,' but he was adamant.

'This is their marriage,' said my dad. 'You can't deprive a man of his children.' Divorce wasn't an option. You had to try and make things work, whatever the circumstances. Everywhere in those days demanded that the wife be subservient to the husband, and it's still going on today, believe me. Women the world over are still second-class citizens. I'm sorry if that sounds harsh but even in the twenty-first century the attitude in many places is that we are here to produce children and satisfy our husbands.

I resented my dad greatly for what he said, but instead of being angry with him, I felt sad. There you go; he was just another man. And I've never quite shaken off the feeling of doom and despair his words instilled in me. To this day when things are going wrong I say to myself, 'You've made your bed, now you must lie in it.'

Chapter Ten

Don't Touch Me

Gerald and me at my sister's wedding, 1970

That evening in Ladywell I sat my father down and told him about everything that had happened. He was shocked, but when it came to me telling him about Gerald's gambling, of course I was talking to a gambler so that didn't do me a huge amount of good. However, my father did write to Gerald asking him how he could behave in such a terrible fashion. Gerald responded with his own letter. In it he admitted he was to blame and said that if I didn't go back he was going to give the house up because he couldn't bear to live there on his own.

This was a nice bit of blackmail, I realised. We had

fought and struggled to get Joan Crescent and he knew how much it meant to me.

'What I want you to do is go back to him and tell him everything you have told me. Tell him how unhappy you are, that you can't go on living this way, that he has to stop this behaviour to save the marriage,' my father said.

'He won't listen, Dad, ' I complained.

'He will,' said my dad firmly. 'You tell him.'

Because there was no room at the house, I moved into a hostel with the boys for a few nights, and then returned home on the following Tuesday.

All the windows were sparkling clean, the beds had been stripped and fresh sheets put on them, the floors had been swept and washed and there was a fire in the grate. It was fantastic. But Gerald was nowhere to be seen and we all had to climb through a window to get in.

That evening, after I had put the children to bed, I was sitting by the fire with a cigarette and a cup of tea when he arrived. Before he could speak, my first words to him were, 'Don't touch me.'

'No, no, no, I'm not going to touch you,' he swore.

'If you hit me I'm going for good,' I told him.

'I promise you I won't,' he said. 'But I want to ask you one question. Did you contemplate going or did you do it on the spur of the moment?'

'Well, I took no clothes with me so it must have been on the spur of the moment, but if you hit me again, I'll go forever.'

Again he promised, swearing on his life he would never do that again. So we sat in that room by the fire till five in the morning, talking and talking and talking. He said he would give up the photography business and get a decent job. 'Honestly, everything will be fantastic,' he said. And sure enough, within a couple of days he'd got a job, working the lump, as they called it, cash in hand for labouring. So that was his money and the Social was mine.

Of course the gambling continued and I learnt how to stretch a pound note like it was elastic, believe you me.

As the years passed I came to understand that when he had money to gamble, he was happy. And if I didn't answer back, everything was fine. I learnt to keep my mouth shut, not argue, and in the process gave up my identity. I became somebody he had nurtured, I realise that now.

Previously I'd been self-assured, but that had gone. I had no confidence and no self-esteem. So he got his way.

In 1963 I fell pregnant for my fourth son Gerald. Towards the end of the pregnancy, Kevin was knocked down by a car while playing outside in the street. It wasn't too serious, but Kevin had this gaping wound on his forehead, and when I saw it I collapsed. I don't know what happened but I started to lose blood and the midwife was called. She told me every-thing was fine but I later found out that it wasn't; for some reason, maybe because of the trauma of seeing Kevin in such a state, the afterbirth was becoming separated from the baby.

This was the one time I wanted Gerald to be there to witness the birth of one of our children, but complications set in, and when young Gerald was born on 28 October that year, he wasn't in the room.

I don't know whether they put me out or I passed out, but I remember coming to and these people were saying to me, 'You're all right now, Mrs O'Dowd, you've had a little son.'

'What are you doing here?' I asked. While I was out an ambulance had been called and a doctor had arrived. The midwife was still there but there was no Gerald.

'Where's my baby?' I cried.

'Well, he was a little blue so we had to give him some oxygen. He's fine,' they told me. They then gave me the little baby, who I christened Gerald Francis in honour of my father. He was also a bit jaundiced, but he had all his fingers and toes, and I cried tears of joy that he had made it and would be OK.

I was absolutely exhausted and fell back into a deep sleep. When I next awoke, there was Gerald with a cup of tea for me, crying. He told me that the ambulance had been called in case I needed to be rushed to hospital, and that the situation had become so serious during the birth that they had nearly lost me.

'No more babies,' he said to me. 'That's it. You're having no more. I don't ever want to go through that again.'

As the months went on, as I recovered and my new baby grew, the constant arguments over money began to wear me down again. Gerald was still working on the lump but I never saw a penny of his wages, didn't even know how much he earned. There was I, feeding and clothing him and the kids and keeping the house together on thirteen pounds a week. I told him I thought it was unfair that I never got to see any of his wages, unlike other wives I knew.

'Don't be greedy,' he'd snarl. 'My money is nothing to do with you. I work for it, so it's mine.'

When little Gerald was about a year old there was one night when we started in on each other again, this time in the kitchen. It was about half nine and the kids were all in bed. He was so vitriolic towards me, calling me all manner of names, that I said to him, 'Why did you marry me? If you're that unhappy, why don't you walk away? Just go. We'll be all right. You can come and see the children any time you like, but if I make you this angry maybe you'd be better off without me.'

The idea of us being apart seemed to anger him all the more. He went for my throat. I was screaming at him to stop and shouted that I'd had enough, that this time I was going to leave him.

At that point he flipped and got hold of a carving knife. Gerald terrorised me with that knife for ten full minutes. It felt like ten years. He held it to my face and told me that he'd cut me up if I said another word.

I was terrified. He called me a fucking cow and told me to keep my mouth shut. 'Nobody leaves me!' he shrieked as he waved the knife back and forth across my face. 'I'll cut you from ear to ear! No one will recognise you! It doesn't matter where you go, I'll find you!'

He would walk away then he'd come back and start again, his voice at a higher pitch. He terrorised me that night like never before. I really thought he was going to kill me. Eventually I scurried under a worktop in the kitchen and screamed, 'Please, please, please go 'way! Go 'way! Go 'way! I want my mum, I want my mum!' At that he dropped the knife to the floor. I was trembling with fear and almost gibbering. He shouted that he was the one doing the leaving.

'OK! OK!' I cried. 'But please don't come back!'

With that he stormed out, off to his mother's in Burrage Road. After I had made sure he had gone I quietly went to bed and put a chair to the door in an attempt to stop him entering the room. I lay there all night, shaking with fear, but he didn't come back.

I had put the children to bed earlier, so none of them witnessed it, and whether they heard or not I don't know. I guess they must have done. I know they talked to each other about the rows but he was careful never to inflict violence upon me in front of them.

People have asked me why I never called the police on him, and I didn't, not once, until late on, ironically over our final row. But that was many, many years later. For the vast majority of our time together, I didn't want the police involved because I was in such a state of panic and fear I was utterly convinced that he meant what he said. It didn't occur to me to go to the neighbours or anybody else.

When he held that knife at my face I saw pure hatred in his eyes. Whatever he had put me through previously, I realised then that I hadn't taken on board what a monster he had become, and the lengths he would go to.

The next morning I took the kids to school and when I came back there was a letter on my pillow on the bed. I read it, sobbing my heart out. In it he begged for my understanding, writing about how dreadful his upbringing had been, how he had been ill-treated and beaten by his uncles. 'Nobody cared about me, I wasn't even allowed to go to my sister's wedding when I was a child,' he wrote.

I thought to myself, 'God bless us and save us, this poor man had such a terrible childhood. Maybe that's why he's like he is, because people were so cruel to him.' There I was, crying for him! Can you believe it?

At four o'clock that afternoon he knocked at the door. I opened it and there he was, head down. 'Is it all right if I come in?' he asked meekly.

'Yes, of course it is,' I said.

Once inside his first question was, 'Did you read my letter?' He didn't apologise.

I told him I had.

He said, 'What do you think? Will you give me another chance? That is the only thing I can think of that is the reason for the way I am.'

I told him I didn't understand. His upbringing wasn't my fault and I didn't think I did anything to provoke him. 'I can't see what I am doing to make you act like that,' I said. 'We had an argument over money. Couples do that all the time. What possessed you to pull a knife on me?'

'You said you were going to leave me,' he cried.

I explained to him that I'd only said it in the heat of the argument. If he'd have said to me, 'Please don't leave; let's sit down and talk,' we could have worked things out. 'I can't describe what I saw in your eyes,' I told him. 'And you want me to stay with you?!'

'I'm begging you,' he said. 'I'll die if you leave me. I'm not going to ask you to forgive me because I wouldn't forgive me. But please don't leave.'

We had turned a corner. This was a different approach. Before the knife incident he'd never have made such a plea from the heart. He'd run out of promises that the violence would never happen again. He'd broken those too many times, so he knew I wasn't going to believe that.

All I could say was, 'Well, let's see what happens.' And you know what? We went to bed and he expected me to perform. I told him to leave me alone for a few days.

I asked his Aunt Kitty whether he'd been cruelly treated as a child. She said there was no truth to it, and she had no reason to lie to me; he'd beaten me in front of her once.

After another few nights with no physical contact in bed he started to become angry with me again, and I was too frightened to say no. So, OK, rather than be punched, I let him do what he wanted. There was no affection there at all. Night after night I gave my body to this man who was now unrecognisable from the person I had fallen in love with just a few years before.

Chapter Eleven

I Know Where to Hit You, My Girl

Taken when I won a prettiest barmaid competition in 1958

By the mid-1960s I was still only in my twenties but I felt ages older. I was utterly exhausted: physically, not least because I'd had five children in seven years. David was born at home on October 13 1964, just 11 months and two weeks after I'd had Gerald.

The birth was incredibly easy – I'd say it took about 20 minutes, certainly no more then 30 – and he looked the dead spit of Georgie. I feel terrible that I exclaimed to the midwife: 'Oh not another boy! I wanted a girl!' because David was (and is to this day) lovely, always happy-go-lucky and easy to get along with.

Because of their proximity in age, he and Gerald were very close, almost like twins, and just like the rest of my children they always looked out for each other.

I struggled to make ends meet throughout that time, but more importantly mentally, because of the strain of my life with Gerald.

The beatings became a regular occurrence and I got used to saying I'd walked into a window when I was asked in the shops about the bruises on my face. The worst thing about the situation was that, before he pounced, he would tell me, 'I know where to hit you, my girl. Remember, I was a boxer so I know where to punch and not leave a mark.'

Even if that wasn't true, it put the fear of God into me hearing those words. I realise now that I was very, very depressed but in those days you didn't talk to anybody about your problems, and if you did mention such things to your doctor, he'd most likely tell you to buck up your ideas.

At first I had put it down to Gerald's insecurity, but then I was in such a state of confusion I didn't know what to think. As I've said, my love was based on absolute loyalty, even to a man who beat me. And afterwards he'd be so sorry, telling me that it was down to the treatment he received from the girl in the army or blaming it on something else entirely. So I'd say to myself, 'Maybe it happened because I talked to that chap. He's so insecure over that girl so maybe I should have realised that and not provoked him.' I actually started to question my own sanity and contemplated suicide loads of times, because I felt I had let my mother, my sister and my kids down. I thought maybe they'd all get on better without me.

I wanted him to stop and think about what he was doing to us. We could have had a fantastic life together but he seemed hell-bent on destroying the prospect of any happiness on the horizon. Sometimes it wasn't just a whack in the face; there'd be his bullying, screaming and shouting for hours. That's just as damaging. It was mental torture. I felt sometimes I'd rather he gave me a slap so then it would all be over.

It also had an effect on the atmosphere in the house as the kids grew. They'd see him ranting away, and before I knew it the boys were at each other and I was constantly trying to pacify them.

I learnt very young that there's no point in arguing with somebody who has lost control of their temper. So I'd just let Gerald go on and on and on until he was spent. But even then he'd try and convince me it was my fault. He had been very clever in isolating me; I only had Heather next door. She was a great ally, but beyond that I didn't have anybody else to confide in. I'd tried talking to my parents, but that had got me nowhere.

One of the worst things was the way he made me feel about sex and about my own body. To this day I refuse to go into the way he treated me in bed, out of respect for my grandchildren who may read this. But believe me, his behaviour in the bedroom was just as bad as the physical and mental abuse I suffered at his hands. Although I was repulsed by him and demanded to be left alone, he would have none of it, refusing to use condoms, as ever, and so, in 1966, I fell pregnant again.

A ray of hope came when he launched his own building company. At least he'd be working for himself, and not forever raving about his employers and the jobs he had to do, or so I thought. I encouraged him as much as I could, and he got a contract with the big building company Wickes.

Money started to come in, and I was allowed to buy little bits and pieces for my house. When Siobhan arrived on 9 November 1967, I was over the moon that I had finally had a daughter, and hoped and prayed that it would make a difference to him. I really did think he would be cock-a-hoop, but he didn't show any more interest in her than he did the boys. I never saw him sit her on his lap or engage with her like a true father would. That hurt me, and also her, I think. She was always wanting to be around him, like little girls are with their dads, but he was quite dismissive. 'Not now, love, in a minute. Daddy's busy,' he'd say, and you'd see the disappointment and confusion in her eyes.

At that time I didn't see a lot of my family, though my father came to visit us at Joan Crescent one Christmas, bringing with him my sisters Teresa and Marie, who I hadn't seen for donkey's years. It was a lovely time; my dad won a turkey at the pub, plucked it and cooked it for us, and for once Gerald was on his best behaviour. Don't get me wrong, there were times when we were a happy family, but there was always the eggshell walking, wondering when it was going to end.

Then he was given this great big Alsatian by his brother-in-law and brought it home. I'd been upstairs waving off Hilda – a neighbour who had helped me with Gerald's home delivery – and when I went downstairs and opened the door to the front room I was confronted with a deep, vicious-sounding growl. Gerald had put the bloody thing in there without telling me a word about it!

I flew back up the stairs. 'There's a big Alsatian in the front room,' I shrieked.

'Yeah,' he said calmly. 'His name's Louis. They can't have him in the pub anymore so I'm taking him.'

I couldn't believe it. 'Gerald,' I said, 'we can barely afford to keep the kids, never mind an Alsatian. I'm scared of it; I don't like it.'

But he was insistent about Louis, and I have to say that in time I grew to quite like that dog. He was only aggressive because of the way he'd been treated by his previous owner, so when we took him in he started to behave. The guy that had owned him came round one night and I saw him slap the dog across the nose, so I knew why he had been vicious.

In the end we had Louis for fourteen years, and as soon as he died, what did Gerald do? Go and buy another one, even though I begged him not to. Heineken was a total lunatic, barking all the while. It never stopped.

Then, when Gerald's sister and her husband moved down to the country, he took in their boxer dog. Again, we couldn't afford it. 'It's going to cost about fifteen pounds a week to keep that dog, and money's tight,' I said. I was expected to pay for him out of the housekeeping and also take him for walks. But he wouldn't listen. This was what upset me most: he would bring these animals home but then I would be expected to look after them, along with the rest of the family.

As it turned out, my expectations that he would change after Siobhan was born were dashed. He seemed to get worse again, and it began to have an impact on my mental health, after years of slaving and abuse and being at his beck and call.

In August 1969 I lost my dad. His lungs were in a terrible state from repeated bouts of pleurisy he'd suffered as a child. We were always told he'd suffered it five times before he left school. Apparently at the time they had thought it was TB. Even when he was close to death, during his last days in hospital in Birmingham, he made up a song for the staff looking after him, taking the mickey out of the size of the portions of food they served:

A million nurses every day
Open a tin of beans a day
And say, 'One, for you . . . and one for you . . .
    and one for you . . .'

Though my dad knew he was dying he was always laughing and cracking jokes in that hospital. The nurses loved him for it.

Within a matter of months of my father's passing, my sister Marie died at the age of twenty-three under the most dreadful circumstances. She had always been frail and sickly, and was tiny. She looked about twelve years old. She was being taken to hospital to have a clot removed from her leg, but the ambulance broke down and they were stranded in freezing conditions. Already that winter was shaping up to be one of the coldest on record, and by the time she arrived at hospital she had hypothermia, it was later discovered. After she came out of hospital she met our sister Kathy for lunch and complained of feeling cold. She had the shivers. Kathy put her in a taxi back to the flat she shared with a couple of girls. The next thing we knew was that one of her flatmates had become so worried that they had called an ambulance and she had been rushed back into hospital.

She succumbed to the flu epidemic which claimed a lot of lives over the winter months that year. I'd just received a letter from her saying she was coming to visit me in London when I got a call from Teresa's husband Barry. When he said he had bad news I thought it was my mam. 'No, it's Marie,' he said. 'She's in a coma and they don't think she'll come out of it.'

Immediately I caught a train to see her. The bottles under the bed contained such an amount of muck from her lungs the doctors were convinced she had been a smoker, even though she had never touched a cigarette in her life. It was horrific. And terribly sad. She died within a couple of days.

Losing my father and sister so rapidly may well have contributed to one of the most saddening incidents of my life. It was triggered by, of all things, Gerald's refusal to move a bag of cement he'd left between the kitchen and bathroom doors. He would always fill the house up with his builder's tools and everything else that came with the job. But that stupid cement was to set into action an escalation of events which would be deadly serious.

I'd been on at him to move the cement for ages, but I should have known. If you ever asked anything of him, he would always take his time. 'I'll do it in a minute,' he'd say. Yet another form of control, I suppose.

So this particular day I decided to move the hefty bag myself. As I bent down to pick it up, I felt something in my back go pop and there was this excruciating pain. I was doubled up, stuck.

He stood over me. 'What have ya done?' he demanded aggressively.

'I've hurt myself,' I said. 'Don't touch me; I'm in agony.'

I painfully climbed the stairs and tried to make myself comfortable in my room. I was in such pain that I couldn't even go to the toilet properly. Lying on the bed I'd put one leg on the fireplace and go in a bucket there; that's how bad it was.

Finally Gerald sent for the doctor, who ran some tests and said, 'You've pulled a muscle, but apart from that I think you've got a kidney infection. You might have to go into hospital.' In the meantime he gave me some medication to calm the inflammation in my back and told me to rest up. Once that was resolved he would look into the kidney infection, he said.

After a disturbed night, Gerald left the house the following morning. With the kids at school and Siobhan barely two years old, a toddler, I was left alone all day, stranded on my back in bed. When Richard got home from school that afternoon he made me a cup of tea and a bit of toast. 'Where's Dad?' he asked.

'I don't know,' I said, even though it was clear to me that he was in the betting shop; he spent all day there.

At six o'clock in the evening he finally came home, and Richard hollered upstairs that Dad was going to make some tea. I lay there waiting, but nothing materialised. He didn't come up to see me, call up and ask how I was. Nothing.

My despair, after nine hours on my own, in agonising pain, knew no bounds. I'd lost my dad and my little sister and now Gerald was acting as if nothing had happened. I felt I'd finally hit rock bottom. I couldn't see how anything in my life could ever get better. I wanted my children to be safe and that night I remember thinking, 'If I die now, they'll give my kids to somebody really nice, people who

can look after them and get them away from him.'
There seemed to be no other way out. I reached onto
the bedside table and grasped the medication the
doctor had left, along with some aspirins, anything I
could get my hands on, and took the lot.

I woke up in hospital several hours later having
my stomach pumped. Apparently Gerald had found
me unconscious and dialled 999.

The next morning I was visited by one of the
hospital psychiatrists, who told me he had spoken
with Gerald. 'Your husband tells me that you have
lost control of the family,' he said. 'I understand that
you leave the children up and running around till all
hours of the night, that you have no time for him
and that you don't spend any time together as a couple
or pay him attention.'

I could not believe my ears, and my fury started
to mount. 'So you're supposed to be a psychiatrist,'
I said, my voice shaking. 'I'm the one who has just
taken an overdose, yet you have decided to believe
everything that man has told you?'

'I've no reason to disbelieve him,' said the doctor.

'Well I'll tell you what you can do then,' I said.
'Turn on your heel and fuck off.' I'm not one for
swearing but I really meant it.

'I beg your pardon?' he said.

'Fuck off,' I said. 'But before you go you'd better
understand that I will never do this again – never,
ever. You can be sure of that.'

So the psychiatrist left, and that evening Gerald

came to visit. With barefaced nerve he confirmed what the doctor had told me, that he had said the kids ran riot and I had no time for him.

'That's a lie, Gerald,' I said, really mad. 'You didn't tell him how you spent all day in the betting shop, did you? You don't give a shit about the kids. I bathe them, I feed them, I play with them, I talk to them about their homework and we wait until you get home. But from now on they're going straight to bed.'

And that's what I did. Driven by the anger his betrayal instilled in me, I got back home and instituted a new regime. The children went to bed every night early and soon enough he'd roll in and ask, 'Where are the kids?'

I coldly told him, 'Hold up, it was you complaining to the doctor that the kids were up when you got home. You come and go as you please; we spend no time together, and then I go upstairs and am expected to perform, and that's it. As long as we are all doing what you want you're happy.'

Somehow, there'd been a subtle shift in our relationship. Whether it was the fact that I'd had a daughter which gave me that courage, I don't know, but it had taken me ten years to reach this point. All I know is that I was at the end of my tether, but at least now I understood suicide wasn't the answer. Because I hadn't died, the only way was up. There is truth in the adage that what doesn't kill you makes you stronger. In my heart and soul I thought, 'Thick or thin I'm going to see this through.'

Chapter Twelve

You Just Couldn't Best Him

*We got there in the end: George, me,
Siobhan, Kevin and Gerald,
Westgate 1970*

As the kids grew up, we all became his slaves. He'd get home and sit in front of the telly, keeping up a constant series of demands. 'Where's my tea? Fetch me this, fetch me that. Here, boy, put the kettle on . . .' In the main he would attack me verbally or physically when the children weren't around, or at least out of the room. But they knew when something was up.

I'd be sitting there recovering from one of his rants and they'd ask, 'What's the matter, Mam?' I'd say that nothing was wrong, but whoever it was would say, 'Mam, I can tell. Has he been having a go at you?'

I'd say, 'Well, he started to row but everything is fine now.'

Georgie would say repeatedly, 'I don't know why you don't leave him.' But having come so far with him – and the line 'You've made your bed . . .' nagging at the back of my head – I couldn't. I read cases in the paper where the children of separated parents went off the rails and thought, 'I don't ever want to put my kids through that.'

There was one particular afternoon when another shred of respect for him was torn from me. Luckily his brother was visiting. Kevin had been naughty, climbing a tree he shouldn't have in the garden, yet rather than just tell him off, Gerald totally overreacted. I don't know whether he was embarrassed that his kids seemed out of control in front of his brother, but he grabbed little Kevin, dragged him upstairs and took his belt to him. I was screaming for him to stop and eventually his brother wrestled the belt from him and his rage subsided. But to me he looked like a wild animal, somebody I couldn't trust to be close to my kids.

This was an unusual event. Gerald would give the boys a clout if they were naughty, but he never overstepped the mark. It seemed he reserved his particularly vicious beatings just for me, and maybe I absorbed that violence so he wouldn't inflict it on our children.

They say in a relationship there's a giver and a taker. Well I took very little. I wouldn't ask for money from him even when he was running his business; I'd rather go out and scrub floors and earn it myself. I wouldn't beg after he told me several times, 'You can't have any more money. You've got your family allowance and your job. Don't be greedy.'

He could give it to the betting shop but not to me.

Although I was growing to despise him, I still couldn't overcome my fear. In those days there'd be tallymen all over our area selling things from door to door, and one time I bought some sheets from one of them on tick, paying from the back door, where, as it turned out, our new washing machine was on view. When the tallyman appeared the following week for the next payment, Gerald was in. As Gerald paid him, the bloke made some passing comment about the washing machine and went on his way.

I heard the front door slam. 'How did that geezer know we had a new washing machine?' he screamed. 'He's been in the house, hasn't he?'

When I said that no such thing had happened he summoned Heather from next door to check my story out. Heather said, 'Of course he wasn't in here. I saw Dinah pay him from the back door, so he must have seen it then.'

She left, and Gerald started to rail against her, claiming that, because she had smiled when he questioned her, she was lying to give me an alibi.

It all seemed so crazy, even for him. 'You're imagining things now,' I said, and just as I finished the sentence he punched me full in the face.

I flew across the room, the back of my head smashing against the windowsill. I remember actually seeing stars – just like they do in cartoons – before passing out for a few minutes. This must have really panicked him because he ran next door crying to Heather, 'I've gone and done it this time! I've killed her!'

She came in and helped revive me, casting black looks at him as he stood there wringing his hands and crying about how it was a mistake; he hadn't meant to hit me.

I was a little dazed for a few days, but the thing about this incident was that another person had been privy to it. Heather started to beg me to leave him. 'Look, Dinah, you can't let him do this to you. You have to stick up for yourself.' But I couldn't see any way out, with no money of my own and six children in tow. Even though I felt the need for independence growing in me, physical fear overshadowed it, particularly since his behaviour left me completely flummoxed. He would be stable for a few months before exploding inexplicably.

Heather was a great friend, and persuaded me to tell Gerald that from now on, we two and our other neighbour Rosemary Foley would be going to the pictures every Friday night so that us girls could have our own time together, but nine times out of ten he'd sabotage it by arriving home far too late for me to make it. Heather's husband Jimmy worked for him, and when they got home late it was as if he'd calculated it to spoil our evening. It was just one night a week, but he begrudged me even that.

I didn't make a big fuss, but thought to myself, 'OK then, maybe we'll go next week.' And then the same thing would happen.

Throughout this period I was losing myself in books; I must have read every Catherine Cookson. The heroines were all bashed about and subjected to terrible things by the men in their lives, but eventually they triumphed. I identified with them. Even though the stories were fiction, there was truth to them. I remember reading *Scream Quietly or the Neighbours Will Hear* by Erin Pizzey, the champion of battered women who came up with the idea of women's refuges. It's more of a booklet made up of conversations with abused women and their children. In it was a story about a fourteen-year-old boy who found the strength to pick up a fridge and hurl it at his father when he beat his mother. Reading that made me think, 'Oh God, it's not just me.'

Although I was very scared of Gerald, I was always capable of feeling sympathy for him, and felt it deeply when he lost his mother and father around this time. They died within six months of each other. Maggie O'Dowd succumbed to cancer while living with her daughter Josephine at the pub she ran in Mottingham, and soon afterwards George suffered a fatal heart attack at the age of sixty-one.

In 1974 the council finally relented to the pressure I had been putting on them for a bigger house – we were so cramped in Joan Crescent by this stage – and we moved to the top of Shooters Hill near Oxleas

Wood. It was exciting in a big house up on top of
Shooters Hill in Woolwich.

The kids had bigger rooms; Richard and Siobhan
had their own and David, young Gerald, Kevin and
George started off sharing the other. The garden was
lovely – well, for a while at least, until Gerald got his
hands on it and filled it with his chickens and junk.

The kids' personalities were beginning to emerge.
Richard went through a naughty stage but was always
easy-going and got on with people. David and
Siobhan have always been confident and George
showed self-belief from an early age, never scared to
be defiant or protective of me.

Kevin was quieter and a bit more bookish. He
looks like his grandfather George O'Dowd, while
Gerald is the spit of his father, to look at, at least.
Sometimes I cried and wished I'd never given him
that name, or at least switched it so he was Francis
Gerald. He was always the gentlest of my kids; I
called him 'my gentleman'. He was very sporty and
proved his athletic prowess time and again. Later he
undertook one of the toughest races in the world and
completed it, a great achievement. His father was
always watching him because he wanted him to
become a boxer, to fulfil the dreams he could never
realise himself. Young Gerald eventually took it up,
and even though he knocked down a couple of kids
in the ring, you could see his heart wasn't in it. He
didn't have that killer instinct; it wasn't in his nature.

One evening, when he was sixteen, I said to him:

'Look, son, do you really want to be a boxer?' He told me he didn't. So I said, 'Well, don't then.' Young Gerald quit and of course his father fell out with him and wouldn't talk to him for months and months.

In 1973 Gerald got a bigger contract with a charitable organisation called the London and Quadrant Housing Trust, renovating properties around south London, many over Brixton way. The next few years were happier. For long periods he earned large amounts of money, and I was working too. Often this just meant that the bets he put on races rose from ten bob each way to hundreds of pounds on the nose, but things seemed to improve nevertheless.

The kids were growing up and we socialised more; L & Q was a massive organisation so there were lots of functions and parties to attend. Gerald's brother David worked for him so I'd make lovely flowing gowns with my sister-in-law Jan and we'd go to company dances and the like. I've always liked talking to people; it doesn't matter to me whether they are low or high, but Gerald could never do that.

Because of the extra money coming in, at Christmas I'd go overboard. I love that time of year, so out would come all the decorations and the table would be groaning with the amount of food I'd cook. My sister Teresa would come to stay, with her husband Barry and her son Trevor and daughter Vanessa, and we'd sit around the table laughing and chatting. Then, more often than not, for no reason at all Gerald would suddenly get up and stalk out of the room. He wouldn't say anything but the mood would be completely spoiled.

The kids would ask, 'What's up with him?' I'd tell them to leave it for a minute and then he'd come back in and sit down as if nothing had happened.

One of the kids would ask, 'What's the matter, Dad?'

And he'd yell that he was perfectly OK, but the job was done: Christmas dinner was ruined. I'd find out months down the line that somebody had said something which he had misinterpreted. My sister might have been talking generally about a perfectly innocent subject and he'd taken it completely the wrong way and thought she was having a go at him.

Another maddening and spoiling facet of his personality was that he would always get lost on a journey. You'd have to leave two hours ahead of schedule to get anywhere on time. If we had people staying who needed ferrying to Heathrow I'd always advise them to get the train. Sometimes he'd insist on taking them and they'd be dashing for their planes at the last minute.

One memorable journey with my sister from our house in Shooters Hill to West Clandon near Guildford took five hours. I could have been up in Scotland in that time. Every word out of his mouth was an obscenity as he shouted at all the other drivers on the road. He was like a madman. At one point we missed a turn-off at a roundabout and found ourselves on a motorway. I gave him explicit instructions as we turned around at the next junction and headed towards the roundabout again. When we got there, what did he do? Missed it again and back we were on the motorway. Whether he had no sense of direction or did it deliberately I don't know, but at times it was as if he couldn't control his actions.

There were certain incidents when you knew he was acting out of spite. During the 1970s when he had his van, we'd agree to take the kids to the coast on a Saturday. They'd be up bright and early running around, and I'd prepare a picnic and give him a shout about eight or nine o'clock to say that we were ready to go. 'I'll be down in a minute,' he'd say, and the minutes would tick by. Ten o'clock . . . eleven o'clock . . . We'd get to noon and the kids would be over any excitement and I'd be sat there disconsolate.

Only then would he get up and come down, saying, 'Come on, come on, let's go.' So into the van we'd pile and hit all the traffic. Sometimes we'd get to Margate or wherever by teatime, just as everybody was leaving. The children would be tired and fractious and I'd be in a bad mood, but he wouldn't have any of it.

The kids were constantly let down by their dad, which can't have been good for them. Sometimes he would insist that we all go with him when he went fishing. I'd bring games for the kids and he'd go off by himself with his rod. More than once we'd be sitting in the car park as the sun went down and the other families left, waiting for him to return. It would get to ten o'clock and the lights would go off so we couldn't see what game we were playing, so we'd sit there in the pitch black until midnight or even one o'clock in the morning. Then he'd bowl up, saying, 'All right? We all ready to go?'

If I asked where he'd been I'd get a mouthful, so it was easier just to bundle the tired children into the van and head for home.

I'm convinced now that he suffered from Asperger's syndrome. I recently read a book on the subject, *Loving Mr Spock: Understanding an Aloof Lover* by Barbara Jacobs. It's the story of a journalist who met a man with Asperger's, which is a form of autism.

The book explains that many men have certain traits related to Asperger's, but there are some for whom it is full-blown, if you like. And I've no doubt in my mind now that Gerald was one of them. When I closed it I thought to myself, 'My God! This is Gerald. This is him!' I wish I'd had that book thirty years ago. I could have shown it to him and said, 'Look, we can get help.' Like the man in the book, Gerald could be ever so kind. He could meet someone in the street and sit with their children and play with them and talk to them, but he couldn't do that with his own. That is an Asperger's trait.

When he told you something which wasn't quite true – and that happened a lot – Gerald could look you dead in the eye and make it believable, he was so convinced himself. Often I would listen to him and think, 'God, yes, he may be right. Maybe I did or said the wrong thing, so it's my fault.' Those with Asperger's are often highly intelligent, and there's no doubt in my mind he was. He could read up on a subject and absorb all the information, just like that. I always felt that he had brains he didn't use.

For some reason, the bookies held him in thrall, and that was his downfall. I don't know what he was chasing all his life. When I'd say, 'You're throwing good money after bad. You'll never ever beat them,' he would shake his head and say, 'I will.' He truly believed that. There was definitely an addictive, compulsive side to his personality which was fed by the bookies.

He also hated going anywhere on his own. During the years he was working for L & Q he would take any of the kids, David, Gerald, even Siobhan, in his van to the betting shop. They would sit outside for three or four hours as he gambled and gambled. He could never understand it when they didn't want to go, and would give them a fiver to accompany him. To a twelve- or thirteen-year-old, that was a lot of money then, so off they'd trot into the van.

At least it was something he'd admit to. 'I hate going anywhere by myself,' he'd say. We could drive from south London to Birmingham and he would talk all the way, non-stop. Anybody driving another car was a cunt, especially if they overtook him. This was a constant thing, what is now called road rage. To this day I wonder where it came from; I could never get a handle on it.

One day in 1977 his murderous temper got the better of him and he pulled a knife on me again, but this time in front of two other people – my sister Teresa and my niece Margaret. Young Gerald, who was only fourteen at the time, was upstairs in his room, and my niece and nephew Trevor and Vanessa were watching television in the front room.

I don't know what set him off that day. Once again he had probably been listening to our conversation and misinterpreted something one of us had said. He came barging into the kitchen while us three women were chatting, and yelled at me, 'Get out of my way! Get these people out of my kitchen!'

I asked him what was going on but he stormed out, grabbed an ornamental Indian knife from a pair we had bought in Petticoat Lane a few years previously, and rushed back into the kitchen. He held it inches from my body and said, 'I'm gonna fucking kill you!'

I screamed so loudly that young Gerald came rushing down from his bedroom, just in time to witness Teresa confront his father. 'Give me the knife,' she urged. With that his mood switched again and he dropped his hand and gave it to her.

I was beside myself with terror, and heard Teresa as she berated him: 'What on earth were you doing? What would have happened if she had stepped forward? You could have killed her!'

All Gerald could do was shake his head and say, 'I wouldn't have done anything. I was just trying to scare her. I'm sorry.'

Young Gerald then jumped at his father and pushed

him out of the front door, screaming, 'Get out of this house!'

Teresa took me to one side and consoled me. 'You've got to tell somebody. He's dangerous, Dinah.'

In the event she drove me to see my GP, Dr Krishna. It felt good, at long last, to let someone in his position know what had been going on all those years. Dr Krishna urged me to call the police, but once again I decided against that. Although the slaps and beatings continued, he never pulled a knife on me again, though he did once hit me around the back of the head with a plate, which knocked me to the floor.

In 1979 Gerald's brother David died at the age of forty-one from a heart attack after a lifetime's drinking, and his sister Josephine went under similarly tragic circumstances a few years later. I think that's another reason I put things to one side during this period, because I sympathised with what he was going through. I decided to mentally shelve my feelings of grievance towards him, as well as the increasing horror I felt at his selfish and self-obsessed behaviour. But still I had to stand my ground, particularly when he threatened my children. It was unusual for him to do that because he knew I had no fear when it came to their safety.

Even so, once, when David was sixteen, a letter arrived for him. Gerald insisted on seeing it. 'What's it got to do with you?' asked David reasonably. 'It's addressed to me.' Gerald started ranting about the house being his, and when David argued, he punched him straight in the face, laid him out flat.

There was a screwdriver lying on a shelf nearby and I picked it up and jabbed it at him. 'You ever do that again to any of my children and I'll stick you with this,' I swore. Gerald backed off. He knew I meant business. His violent nature seemed to have got the better of him now he had lost all self-restraint. Thankfully he seldom took it out on the children, but they feared him and they certainly didn't respect him, and nor did I.

I remember once asking him, 'Would you not go and see a psychiatrist?'

'I'm not mental,' he said gruffly.

I told him that I didn't mean that, but that a professional might be able to give him some help to find out where his fury came from, and why he didn't react normally to life.

'I am normal; there's nothing wrong with me,' he said.

Chapter Thirteen

That Boy has Something

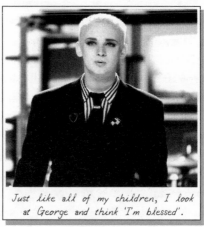

Just like all of my children, I look at George and think 'I'm blessed'.

There's been some lovely photographs of Georgie taken throughout his career; my favourite is of him in a dark suit, collar and tie with white-blond hair. He looks so lovely. I look at it and say to myself, 'Now where did you come from to look so beautiful?' People talk about him, saying that they love him, that he's gorgeous and I still get all protective: 'Ah shut up, he's mine!'

Georgie was very self-contained and would play for hours by himself. He was never part of the rough and tumble but had a lot of female admirers from a very young age, from little girls around where we lived to his school dinner ladies and the staff who looked after the kids in the playground.

I worked as a dinner lady at his school, Eltham Green, so saw how chatty he was with the women there. Can you imagine this charming little boy coming up to you and saying, 'Oh you look lovely,' because you wore make-up? It endeared him to those ladies. He was always on at me: 'Why don't you wear make-up, Mum?' But I wouldn't, not on a daily basis, only special occasions.

George was different; he loved dressing up. I was the same as a kid; I'd take scissors and a needle to clothes and adapt them so they suited me better, and he would do the same, watching how I sewed and stitched, learning from me. George was also very caring and helpful towards other children. If they were in some sort of bother he'd try to help out. If there was a disabled child who was being ignored or not having a good time he was always very concerned.

I have to say that my kids are generally like that. That's the way I brought my children up. I have always hated people being picked on and was worried about my husband's nature coming out in them, so I did my best to instil fairness and understanding into them. Unfortunately my husband's temper would sometimes come out in them when they argued and I'd have to say, 'Calm down, let's discuss this reasonably.' And although Kevin was a quiet lad and very studious at school, he shows something of his father's temper now and then.

George was a very clean child; everything had to be just so. He shared a bedroom with Gerald, who was a typical boy, slinging his clothes on the floor, and he and George had some humdingers. 'He never keeps the room tidy,' Georgie would complain. He had a temper too, and would let fly as often as the rest of them. I was always calming the waters; that seemed to be my job in the house, with my husband and with my kids. I know a decent argument is a good way of clearing the air, but I always wanted to find an easier and less stressful way than ranting and raving. To me, when somebody loses their cool you might as well bang your head against a brick wall. You're never going to salvage anything after that.

Because of his feminine side, his brothers called Georgie 'queer' and a 'poofter' from an early age. When they were all cavilling with each other, that would be the insult they'd sling at him, however much I tried to nip it in the bud: 'Stop that! It's not nice!' Ignorance is a terrible thing, and I think there is a lot of it in macho culture. Rather than sitting down and talking things through, a lot of people prefer to live in ignorance.

Georgie told me he was gay in the kitchen in Eltham when he was fourteen years old. We were on our own in the house and he said he wanted a word:

'You know I'm different to the rest of them, don't you, Mam?'

I always had a special affinity with George, even though we argued like crazy. That wonderful feminine aspect of his nature warmed you to him. He'd fight with you, and then five minutes later would endearingly say, 'Would you like a cup of tea, Mam?'

When he came out to me, I don't know that I had an idea. I remember I cried. I didn't know what gay was, or anything about homosexuality, so I said, 'Well, explain it to me.'

He simply said, 'I like boys instead of girls.'

I could take that on board but I didn't know about the physical implications, and that lack of knowledge disturbed me slightly. But the one thing I did know was that he was my son, through hell and high water. He's what God gave me, and he's mine and I love him, and I don't care what other people think. I know a lot of mothers have disowned their gay sons, but there is no way I would ever have abandoned him. Gerald wasn't surprised when George came out. In many ways you'd expect him to be outraged, but he had a very contradictory nature, and would constantly surprise me. He also knew that I would not tolerate any criticism of my children, scared of him though I was. In fact Gerald took the other boys out for a drive in the van and told them that George was different, and that they should accept him.

I was always amazed at the cleverness of George's arguments, thinking, 'God, this boy's only fourteen years old and he's running rings around me, a woman of forty with six children!' But I would never stop him or any of my kids from expressing themselves.

Of course he encountered a lot of prejudice,

particularly in the 1970s, although to this day I don't know what he went through at school, because Georgie wasn't one for coming home and moaning about the way he'd been treated. He was always being sent home, turning up as he did in kaftans and plat-form boots like Elton John and David Bowie. It's true that we rowed constantly over his appearance. He was forever dyeing his hair, and once I even gave him black dye to cover up some awful bright orange job he'd done himself.

There was one time when he cheeked his father – George would never back down – and Gerald chased him up the stairs. Georgie tripped and banged his head on a radiator. As he was lying on the floor Gerald shouted at him, 'Why don't you stand up and take it like a man?'

George responded, 'So you're a man, are you? Well if you're a man, I don't want to be a man!' And that's where he got the title to his first book: *Take It Like a Man*.

There was another incident when George was in his mid-teens which sticks in my mind. He was sitting on a bench on the corner near the house eating a tomato when these two young girls walked by. One of them said something, and he ended up lobbing the tomato; it caught her right in her face.

The first I knew about this was when her father came round saying that George should be punished. I told him to leave it to me. When I asked George what had happened, he explained the girls wouldn't leave off calling him a poof until he threw the tomato.

So when the bloke called the next day I told him what had happened. 'She had no right to be calling my son names like that. As a father you make sure you tell her off.'

'I certainly won't!' he blustered, demanding again that we punish George, but I sent him away with a flea in his ear and that was an end to it.

Gerald was always supportive of George, and to an outsider his father's attitude may appear out of character, but whatever else he did, Gerald genuinely believed in his children. Also, let's not forget, I would not let anybody say anything about George, and my husband knew that.

At one time we had my sister-in-law May living with us. She was wheelchair-bound and one day George became involved in an argument with the bloke she was with, I can't remember what about. Suddenly the bloke snapped at George: 'Shut up, you little poofter.'

Well, that was it. 'Don't you ever, *ever* say that to my son again,' I said. 'I don't care who you are or how big you are, you say that again and you're out.' When it comes to my children I show no fear.

It is still difficult for me to understand exactly how my husband felt about George and his sexuality. He came from a very masculine environment and was extremely macho, yet he bought tickets for George to see David Bowie in Lewisham when he was just twelve years old, he gave him thirty pounds to go towards George's first pair of bondage trousers from Vivienne Westwood's shop Seditionaries, and time and time again he would jump in the van and go to Georgie's aid if we thought he was in trouble when he moved away from home.

I think George did things Gerald would never have dreamed of doing himself, and I believe he admired his son for that. George never cared tuppence what anybody said, whereas Gerald was always too aware of what others thought about him. Deep down, I believe my husband had no confidence in himself, which is why he was all bluster, whereas George has always had a core of self-belief. It's also possible that Gerald wanted to do the things that George did but didn't have the nerve, so maybe there was a respect there for George's tenacity.

Georgie always had my full support, and I loved seeing him dressed up, helping him along the way by adapting and making clothes for him. When he got those expensive bondage trousers I took a look at the pattern and ran him up another three pairs, one out of Union Jack material he got from somewhere or other.

When Georgie started getting his name in the papers as a punk I took him aside and told him what my father had told us as kids: 'Look in the mirror and find your own faults. Once you know what they are, nobody else can hurt you.' That was the message I gave to all my children.

I asked George whether he cared what people said about him and he shrugged and said, 'No.'

'Are you sure?' I asked him

'Yes, absolutely.'

'OK,' I said. 'If you want to wear this stuff and you genuinely don't care what others say, then go ahead and wear it. It's your life; do what you want with it.'

Of course the next day he came home with his hair dyed blond and we had another row about him going too far. When I shouted at him he simply said, 'Well, you dye *your* hair!' Maybe it goes back to my Dublin roots, where we were all encouraged to dance, sing and entertain. Some mothers would have been disapproving of George's dyed hair and make-up but in the main I loved it, though I did draw the line when he shaved his eyebrows off to look like Bowie at the age of fifteen.

I remember my mother saw Georgie's talent well before the rest of us, when he was just eleven years old. It was one dinnertime when she was staying with us. Again, the kids were all cavilling, some of them calling him a poofter and all that business, and she said, 'Stop it now. Leave him alone.' And then she turned to me and said, 'Listen, Dinah. That boy has something. Nurture it. I heard him singing upstairs. He has such a beautiful voice.'

Sometimes Georgie'd be in his room singing a David Bowie number and I'd swear it was the record. He could do Marc Bolan to a T as well. He definitely has some of my father in him; my dad had a lovely voice and could make up a song about anything. To this day George does the same thing. He'll take a popular song and put silly lyrics to it. It reminds me so much of my dad it's not true. I clearly remember my dad singing one he wrote, called 'If You Ever Go Across the Sea to Ireland':

Last night as I was drinking in the Beamish
It was only at the closing of the day
And I strolled home just after midnight
And me wife she started giving out the pay . . .

It was that kind of wordplay which re-emerged in George's talent, I believe. Maybe I passed something along to him as well, because I was so keen on music, dancing and clothes when I was a kid. To this day my family get up and sing if they're out at a party. It's an Irish thing, isn't it? And George witnessed that from when he was a baby.

Of course, like any mother I was worried when Georgie left home in April 1979. He was just seventeen, and announced that he was going to stay with his friend Martin Degville – who was later in Sigue Sigue Sputnik – in Walsall.

I was OK about it, but only if he agreed to stay in contact with my sister Teresa, who was nearby in Ladypool, and tell her where he was living. I knew she would look after him.

'If ought happens to you, she's there to help, you can go to her,' I told him. And in fact Teresa ended up being the taxi service for George, Martin and all their friends, ferrying them all over the place, going to the Bowie nights at the Rumrunner and the like. George would always win the bottle of champagne because he had Bowie off pat. Georgie also worked with Martin at his stall Degville's Dispensary in the flea market in the Birmingham Bull Ring, where they made and wore all these bizarre outfits.

After several months, Georgie returned to London but didn't come home; instead he lived in a series of squats. I was worried about my boy, and if ever he phoned because he was in trouble, I'd tell Gerald, 'We have to go over. He might be hungry, or someone might be having a go at him.' I'd make sure we got there and took Georgie whatever he needed, food or money. I can't stress enough that Gerald drove me over on many occasions. Those were among the good things that he did, helping me to help our kids along their way.

We got to meet George's mates on the Blitz scene – people like Philip Salon, who was older and clearly cared about him, and Marilyn, who I never had much time for. Then, in 1980, just before George formed Culture Club with Jon Moss, Roy Hay and Mikey Craig, my mam died from cancer at the age of sixty-seven. It was such a shame she never got to witness his success because they loved each other dearly.

She had found it very hard to come to terms with the death of my father and then my sister ten or so years earlier. I only found out a couple of years ago that she had had to make the decision for the hospital to withdraw life support from Marie when she was in her coma. That must have been the most horrendous choice to make and in a way I'm glad I didn't know at the time, because I'd have been screaming for them to keep going. I don't think I could have done it. People do recover from comas, so it would have to be very convincing for me to even get close to making that call. But apparently they told her that the tests showed that Marie's brain was irrevocably affected by her heart having stopped so many times.

The stress of that decision, I believe, brought back the cancer my mother had suffered in her forties. At that time they had put a radium pack inside her which they said would last for fifteen years, and she came up to the end of that period just after Marie died.

Mam could never settle; she went home to Ireland, and then came back to live in Birmingham, where she lived on her own. Eventually my brother Frank persuaded her to go back again to Ireland, and she got a lovely little place with a warden living in the grounds. She was quite happy for a while but when the cancer returned she moved in with Phyllis before entering a hospice. My family in Ireland waited until the eleventh hour before telling me that she was dying. She deteriorated very rapidly and then it was all over. The cancer consumed her.

She would have been cock-a-hoop over Georgie's success. She loved him, and he loved my mam.

*

Culture Club were taken on by manager Tony Gordon and signed to Virgin Records.

I remember the night George rang me and said, 'I'm on *Top of the Pops* tomorrow, Mam.' I got my friend Heather round and we watched him sing 'Do You Really Want to Hurt Me?', dancing around all over the place.

I said to Heather, 'Oh my God, I'm really worried that he'll trip over all those camera cables and wires!'

He rang immediately afterwards asking if I'd seen it. I told him I was so scared about him falling over live on TV and he scolded me: 'Mam, it was recorded yesterday!' I felt a right twit, but what was I supposed to know about how television programmes are made?

Soon George was plastered all over the media. We were delighted for him and he was very generous in return. But there was an unbelievable element to it. Sometimes I'd be sat in the front room with a cup of tea and I'd turn on the television and there he'd be. 'That's Georgie,' I'd have to remind myself.

He bought his father two cars. The morning after the first one arrived there had been a high wind overnight which blew all this white blossom over the bonnet and roof. Gerald could never show gratitude at the best of times and took the first opportunity to carp. He thought the petals were blemishes in the paintwork, and came in moaning, 'I knew it was a crappy old thing! It's all pitted!'

He was convinced until I went out and swept it away with my hand: 'It's the stuff off the tree, you twit!'

Whenever things needed to be done around the house George insisted on paying, but Gerald would always ask via me or Siobhan. He couldn't bring himself to tell George himself that something needed paying for; it was as though he was scared of him.

Soon all these relations of my husband started ringing up, inviting me over for tea or wanting to come round. Lots of people who had passed me by when I first met Gerald started calling me. I was pretty quick off the mark though, and politely said, 'Well I'm sorry but I won't be here on that day; I'm going out.'

At this time I had a job at the old people's home Cooper Court but I wasn't about to give it up because I liked my guvnor, my workmates and the people there. One day I went to pick up a prescription for an old girl. The woman at the counter said, 'If my son was on *Top of the Pops* I'd be dripping in diamonds driving round in a Bentley.'

'Would you?' I asked. 'Around Woolwich? I don't think so. People would go, "Look at her. Who does she think she is?" I'm excited for him but he's in a different world from me.'

I took George's fame as part and parcel of life, though I had no idea how famous he was going to become. It was like Beatlemania. He was mobbed all over the world and sacks and sacks of mail arrived daily. It was impossible to get through it all. We'd sit down and read them to each other. One day there was a knock on the door and there stood a guy who had travelled from America especially to take a photo-graph of us, not even George. I said, 'Oh my God, hold up! I've got me washing and ironing to do!'

George was ever so generous to his family, and made us a part of his success, flying us all around the world to watch him in concert. One time he was touring in Europe and flew us over to the French Riviera. We stayed in this fabulous hotel on the front and went sightseeing, to Princess Grace's pink castle and to the casinos in Monaco. I was so shocked to see, amid all the lavishness, with yachts in the harbour and beautiful young girls in bikinis, three alcoholics sat on a bench, really down and out, swigging from their bottles, like you might see in Lewisham or Woolwich.

I couldn't comprehend how such people could exist alongside such luxury, but since then I've been to lots of places thanks to Georgie, and understand that life comes in many different shapes and sizes the world over.

Back at the hotel we dined with the other Culture Club members, and Roy, the bassist, sent back expensive pudding after expensive pudding after just one spoonful: 'Oh, I don't like that.' To me that was sheer waste.

I looked at the menu and exclaimed, 'George! It's twenty-four pounds for a pot of tea!'

'Mam,' he chided me, 'stop worrying about money!'

'Well I wouldn't pay it,' I said. That was the side

of my personality which had had to struggle to make ends meet for years on end, and I couldn't shrug it off lightly. I still dislike that. It's wasteful, totally unnecessary with so many in the world starving.

I was also uncomfortable with being approached all the time by complete strangers. 'Hello, darling, how are you? Your son is sooo wonderful,' they'd say.

'Darling? Who are you? Hold up; you don't even know him.' It's not the real world. What is fame? An imposter, I think.

Meanwhile our house in Shooters Hill was often besieged by press people, asking all sorts of questions and interviewing all of us about every aspect of George's early life. Initially it was great, but we are down to earth people and not that enamoured of fame.

I received a call from a very friendly chap on one of the papers. He said he'd heard that our dog had been knocked down and was enquiring after him. 'No, the dog's fine,' I said.

Soon, very subtly, he had got the conversation onto George but after a few seconds I realised: 'Whoah. Hold up a second. Get lost.'

But the fact that I had talked to him at all gave him licence. There was a big spread in the paper the next day quoting me on all sorts of stuff regarding George. I called the editor: 'How dare you quote me? I never said any of the things you have in that article.'

He said, 'But did you speak to my reporter?'

'Yes, I did. But I'll never speak to him again.'

George said, 'Don't worry about it. It's no big deal. From now on, just say "No comment", and that's it.'

I think the way the whole family coped with George's fame had something to do with my upbringing. In Dublin, if you started showing off, you were soon brought down to earth with a bump: 'Don't start that around here!'

I remember once George was at home after he became famous, and asked Siobhan to make him a bit of toast.

Her response? 'Get up and get it yourself.'

'But I'm a pop star,' he said, tongue in cheek.

'Are you?' she asked. 'What's that got to do with anything? You're just being lazy.'

'I'll give you ten pounds,' he offered.

She took it but said, 'Next time make your own.'

I know that George tried desperately to stay the same person, but it's terribly hard in the face of all that adulation. And of course for the first few years he was everybody's darling and couldn't put a foot wrong.

When they were on the road the band would stay in posh hotels but George wanted to stay with the road crew, because they were more on his level. But his manager would stop him, because stars weren't supposed to behave like that.

And people around here did truly believe that Richard, Kevin, Gerald, David and Siobhan were walking around with their pockets stuffed full of money. 'It gets on my nerves,' they would complain. 'You go up the pub and they're all saying, "Oh, you can buy this round. Your brother's a millionaire."'

I told them, 'Just say, "You're right. He's a millionaire. I'm not."'

Siobhan was still at school and caught in a double bind. If she didn't talk about him she was ashamed of him, but if she did she was bragging. She kept herself to herself, and had a couple of nice friends she stuck with. One of them had a father who said, like many people the first time they saw George on *Top Of the Pops*, 'Oh did you see that beautiful girl? What a lovely voice. You'll have to buy me that record.'

His daughter said, 'It's not a girl, Dad, it's a feller.'

'How do you know?'

'Cos I go to school with his sister.'

'Well, I don't care. He's got a nice voice. Can you get me that record tomorrow?'

In 1983 as the money started to flow in and Culture Club hit big in America, Georgie announced that he was going to give us an allowance. I asked him not to put it in his dad's name because it would go straight to the betting shop. So it went in my name, and my idea was that, out of that money, every bill would be paid: gas, electric, telephone, insurance, the rent. Then I wouldn't have to bother with any of that. I was now working as a cleaner and helper at Cooper Court, sheltered accommodation for the elderly not far from where we lived.

Gerald was still contracted to L & Q, but all of a sudden decided that, even though he knew nothing about the music business, he should control Georgie's career. It was absolutely absurd, and luckily George and Tony Gordon managed to calm him down and show him they knew what they were doing.

In the early years of Georgie's fame I received quite a bit of attention, because my son often mentioned me in the press. Initially, Gerald said he wasn't interested in being interviewed but then he started to say, 'Well I'm not answering questions unless they pay me.' Later Gerald started to claim that Culture Club's success was down to him. He even wore Georgie's cast-offs. They looked ridiculous on a burly middle-aged builder. I remember he walked in one day in a pair of Boy boots with studs all over them. I don't know how we all didn't wet ourselves, they looked so comical.

'What do you mean?' he snapped when he caught us exchanging furtive glances. 'He was gonna throw them out but they're still all right to wear.'

One day in 1983 we were arguing again. I don't know what I'd said – probably nothing as usual – and Gerald went to raise his fist. In a flash, because we'd had so many journalists around, interviewing us and asking questions about Georgie, I said to Gerald, 'Go on then, hit me again. Another one won't make any difference to me but it will to you. Tomorrow it'll be all over the papers.'

That day he raised his fist to me for the last time.

I guess I was happy that I would suffer no more physical pain, but this was when he introduced a far more insidious form of abuse into our relationship: mental cruelty. He'd always been on at me but this was when he upped the ante, deriding everything I said or did, sneering at me and my friends, undermining my personality as the gambling took over his life now that there was more money around. I began to feel just as cornered as when he had punched and kicked me to the floor, even though this was a time when he should have been so happy at our son's success.

Chapter Fourteen

Heading for Deep Water

The three of us in Chinatown, New
York, 1984

While I was dealing with Gerald's moods and
tantrums I started to become aware that George might
be heading for deep water. All our lives George and
I have had great conversations, because we have got
on so fabulously. OK, we argued like cat and dog,
but we were still talking to each other. Then, suddenly,
he stopped communicating with me, and I knew
something was up.

I was in hospital for a week or so in the mid-1980s
after having had a hysterectomy. Although a big
bouquet of flowers arrived, he didn't visit me once. I
was very surprised and alarms bells started ringing in
my head. I said to Siobhan, who was already doing bits

and pieces for him, like running errands, looking after his accounts, making sure his dry cleaning was picked up, 'This is very unusual. He's not even phoning me.'

A couple of days later, when I was almost fully recovered, a nurse came and told me he'd called and asked the doctor if it would be OK for me to travel to him to Switzerland, where he was recording with Culture Club and had also started work on a book. I liked the idea of that; Switzerland is where everyone gets well, isn't it? I was delighted.

When I came out of hospital we spoke, and he organised for me to take the scenic route – boat to the French coast and then by car with Billy Button, his assistant at the time. But the boat ride was awful – the English Channel was particularly rough that day – and Billy's decision to bring his girlfriend with him meant that she took over the back seat of the car. The whole journey was really uncomfortable.

Anyway, we finally got to our hotel late in the evening, and I spoke to George and arranged to go and see him at the house where he was staying the next morning. He opened the door with a cigarette in his hand. He'd never smoked before, so when I asked him why he was now, he snapped, 'I'm writing my book!'

Then he started rabbiting on, talking in a way which was totally out of character. He also looked strange. There was no eye contact, which I hate.

As we chatted I looked around the room, and on a table was a toilet roll with cling film over the top and a hole pierced in it. I picked it up. 'What's that for?' I asked.

'Put it down! Put it down! It doesn't belong to you!' he shouted.

Walking towards the kitchen I saw all these pipes lying around, and then came across what looked like half an Oxo cube. 'What's that?' I asked.

He snatched it out of my hand. 'Mum, will you just sit down and stop snooping! This all belongs to the guy who owns the house, all right?'

I sat down and said to him quietly, 'Something's wrong, George.'

Again he went off: 'Mum, there's nothing wrong! OK, I'm smoking. What's wrong with that?'

I challenged him: 'You haven't phoned me. You won't look at me when I talk to you. Something is up.'

He would have none of it. We had something to eat and he kept up this barrage to Billy: 'Take her here, take her there. Buy her whatever she wants.'

I was whispering to Billy, 'I don't want anything. All I want to do is talk to my son, and for him to talk to me.'

I never got the opportunity during that trip. He was in the studio a lot, so we'd have meals together, but he wasn't right; his talk was too rapid.

One day in Switzerland I could hear all this screaming and shouting coming from the bedroom. George and Jon Moss were having a massive row over a T-shirt Mossy believed George had taken. Eventually he made George tip his suitcase out to look for it. They were raging at each other. I couldn't believe, with all the thousands of pounds swilling about, that they could both lose it so badly over a bloody T-shirt.

The next day Siobhan – who had already been over there helping George out – and I caught a flight with Mossy back to England while his father returned by car. When I got back there was no change – no phone calls, no nothing. Something was up but I couldn't quite put my finger on it. When I talked to Gerald about my concerns, he just couldn't see it. 'What d'ya mean?' he'd ask. I later found out Siobhan knew that drugs were getting a grip on George, but she couldn't tell me because she thought it would upset me too much.

It started to become horrendous. George and Marilyn went off to Jamaica where I think they got seriously out of it. It was clear by then that he was in deep trouble, but I could never get hold of him to confront him; barriers were always placed in my way and he holed up in his mews house in Abercorn Place, St John's Wood.

One day at work I became so upset that I told my workmates Phyllis and Wilma, 'That's it. I'm going to St John's Wood,' and went straight to the station at Woolwich Arsenal.

When I rang on his door it was obvious there were people inside; I could see movement behind this Japanese screen he'd put up, but they wouldn't let me in. Philip Salon's flat overlooked Georgie's, and he kept on shouting down to me, 'He's in there Mrs O'Dowd.'

'Get back inside, Philip. Shut your window!' I shouted back.

I got on the intercom and said, 'I know you're there, George. I'm not going until you let me in, and I'll scream and shout and bang on the door and make a real show of you till you do.'

Eventually, after about half an hour, George came to the door. I was absolutely floored at his appearance. He was totally out of it, so thin, wearing a pair of size ten white jeans encrusted with diamante. I don't think his waist was even twenty-six inches.

I went in, and in the gloom I could just make out two people sitting around: his so-called friend Hippie Richard, and another feller. On the floor was a big bag full of banknotes. The place was a mess. 'What's going on, son?' I asked, but he was too far gone to even answer. So I pointed at the two fellers and said, 'You and you. Out of here *now*! And don't come back!' I picked up a cricket bat which was lying on the floor and yelled, 'If you don't get out now I'll batter the heads off you!' Of course they fled.

George managed to muster, 'You can't talk to my friends like that!'

'They're not your friends,' I told him. 'Look at the state of you, son.' I pushed him in front of the mirror. 'Now you tell me you see a healthy young man,' I said.

'I look all right,' he snapped defiantly.

After they left his mood changed, and I realise with hindsight that he had taken another snort upstairs without me knowing because he became cock of the walk. Down he came. 'Mum, Mum, sit down and I'll make you a cup of tea,' he said, the voice of reason, talking to me as though his life was totally together and that I shouldn't worry. 'There's nothing wrong with me. I'm fine, honestly.'

I wasn't having it and set about clearing the place up over the next three or four hours. While I was there he phoned his friend Bonnie, an American who was one of his biggest fans and became one of his closest friends. 'Bonnie, I want you to come here tomorrow and clean the house from top to bottom,' he said, and then turned to me. 'See, Mum, I'm getting it sorted. Everything is back under control.'

Of course I believed it, because I wanted to and also because drug addicts are very plausible people. They can switch from being totally zonked to appearing capable in the extreme.

That period in our lives was awful, particularly since one of the things he had first become famous for was his anti-drugs stance. I never in a million years thought he'd touch them, because he'd always been such a strong character. It was a terrible shock. Of course the media got wind of what was happening and started hounding him and us. I have to say that now I don't give two monkeys for the press. I know from bitter experience they will write what they want to, not what you've said.

By 1986 things had become so serious that I was in bits, absolute flitters. I now know that George had moved from cannabis to Ecstasy to cocaine and was by this time on heroin. Friends of Georgie's started to die around him – people like the keyboard player Michael Rudetsky, who had come over from America to write songs with George and fatally overdosed one night at his house in Hampstead.

When he had arrived in the country the day before, Michael went missing for hours before turning up at George's house. It was later discovered he had gone to score drugs, having been strip-searched at the airport. That night during a recording session he kept on being sick and George offered to call a doctor but he was insistent that he was all right. So Georgie left him to stay the night in Hampstead and went off to sleep at his other place in St John's Wood. My son Kevin, who was working for Georgie, found him dead the next morning.

George was now avoiding all our calls. He was down to under nine stone and was taking as much as five grams of coke over a weekend as well as three or four grams of heroin a week and anything else he could get his hands on.

One of George's friends, a photographer called David Levine, opened the press floodgates by selling the story about his drug taking to the *Daily Mirror*, and then in July 1986 the *Sun* ran the front-page headline 'Junkie George Has 8 Weeks To Live'. This was sparked by a trip Gerald and I had made across

London to meet this friend of George's who we knew was buying him drugs. I called him and even spoke to his mother, and arranged that we should talk to him at George's home in Hampstead.

He was waiting for us when we arrived but unfortunately we didn't get very far because Gerald lost it, acting stupidly and threatening him, shouting that he was going to kill him. When I tried to calm things down Gerald stormed off to confront George himself at his place in St John's Wood.

When he arrived there had already been a kerfuffle. Apparently a couple who knew George had been banging on the door so loudly that the police had been called.

They'd gone by the time Gerald turned up, and when he gained access, George fled upstairs and locked himself in the bathroom. So what did Gerald do? He bundled together some clothes he found on the living room floor and started three little fires to smoke George out.

Believing there to be a genuine fire, Georgie came out of the bathroom and when he saw what his dad had done, fled to his friend Philip Sallon nearby. George immediately called me in Hampstead. 'Get that fucking lunatic out of my house!' he raged. 'He's set fire to my front room!'

I couldn't believe it: 'Don't be silly George. Your father would never do that.' I said that I'd talk to him and then help George's friend and assistant Bonnie clean up any mess.

When Gerald came back to Hampstead he denied everything, claiming that it was George who had started the fires himself.

But, as Bonnie and I were leaving, Gerald couldn't help himself. 'Well it worked didn't it? I got him out of the house!'

I went cold. 'What are you talking about? You could have killed our son, you maniac!'

After that I refused to talk to him. The three of us travelled to St John's Wood, cleaned the place up and finally returned to Shooter's Hill at 5 o'clock in the morning.

I went to bed while Gerald woke David up to tell him what had happened. Only he didn't give him the truthful version of events. David came into my room as I tried to sleep and said: 'This is no good. This has to stop now. George has tried to burn his own house down.'

He wouldn't listen when I told him that in fact it had been Gerald and left. I slept for a few hours and the next lunchtime idly switched on the TV after making myself a cup of tea.

I couldn't believe it. There was David telling the world that his brother had a serious drug problem which was now threatening his life. It turned out that during the early hours he had gone outside and talked to the press people who door-stepped us constantly at the time. I could see that David was absolutely petrified as he spoke, and George was certainly unhappy about it, saying something to the effect of:

'Isn't it nice when one of your own litter squeals on you?'

But I'm glad now that it happened, because it certainly set Georgie on the road to recovery. Though I wish David had gone about it differently.

It was all becoming an unholy mess. George was arrested a couple of times – once for heroin possession – and appearing in the papers daily as speculation mounted that he might be the next to die. I was beside myself with worry. I used to come home at night and pray to God to save him. I hadn't been to church for twenty-odd years, but now believe returning to my faith gave me the strength to see it through.

I think the turning point for George came when his friend Mark Vaultier died of a heroin overdose, alone at his flat. That night when I went to tell him Mark had gone, George let us into the house in Hampstead. I remember looking at him and thinking to myself that he might die. 'Son, this has got to stop,' I said, sobbing. 'Please, please, you have to stop.'

He looked at me very soberly and said, 'I will, Mum. I promise.'

I think one of the things which most shocked George was the fact that Mark had died all by himself. 'There wasn't a soul with him, Georgie; they just left him,' I said of the 'friends' who had given Mark the heroin. 'That's what'll happen to you. They'll be all over you when everything's fine and you're buying the drugs, but if something happens they'll just walk away.'

I came to understand this better soon afterwards

when George agreed to go into rehab at Meg Patterson's clinic at Mill End House in Oxfordshire. She was recommended by Virgin boss Richard Branson, who had taken a personal interest in George's problems and tried to intervene several times. Meg was renowned for having weaned pop stars and other addicts off drugs, and I'll never forget what she said to me when George first arrived to be connected to her famous Black Box Brain Tuner.

'That's not your son,' she said to me. 'You must understand that his personality has been changed by drugs. If you fell on the floor he'd step over you to get to them.'

Once I'd taken that on board the task for him and us was to get the real George back. This was made more difficult by the fact that he was surrounded by people who were willing to find drugs for him. But he was given strength from within not only by the treatments he had, but also the realisation which hit when Mark died.

For a three-month period I was off work and Gerald and I moved into Hampstead with George to make sure he had as much support as possible. There were also two nurses, one for daytime and the other at night. It would always be down to me to help them coerce George into taking the medication which kept him calm. Maybe it's because I had more stamina, but I would also sit up with George of a night. I didn't care if he was talking nonsense – at least he was communicating – and I tried to always be there to listen.

I remember one evening George came downstairs, shaking. 'I can't take any more of this. I have to go out, Mum,' he said.

I knew what he meant. 'So you're going out to buy drugs, are you?'

He looked dumbfounded. 'Oh Mum . . .'

'Well,' I said, 'I don't have much money in my purse, maybe eight pounds, but you might as well take that so you can buy as much as possible. Go on. Go and get it. Kill yourself. Go on.'

He looked close to tears. 'I don't want to, Mum,' he whispered.

'Now make your mind up,' I said. 'Look, son. Only you can do this. I can only be here for you, to prop you up and listen to you. I'll stay awake all night talking to you. Tell me what it is that is making you take this stuff.'

He said that he really didn't know, but I think it was the break-up with Jon Moss which had been the final straw. The pressures of fame are enormous, even for a strong personality like George, but I think he was badly affected by the failure of his relationship with Jon.

As part of George's recovery, he started to work again. After three months – once I was satisfied that he was overcoming his illness – I moved back to Shooters Hill and Gerald stayed on with him in Hampstead for a while longer, helping out as he started to go back on the road and make personal appearances to launch his solo career. I asked him to take his father along with him on promotional trips to Europe so that they could bond a bit more. I wanted Gerald to see that George needed and wanted him, and for a time it worked.

I thought the press were very cruel. The stories about George were extremely derogatory, and there was no need for it. Some even claimed he had Aids; it was absolutely disgusting. They had us surrounded in our own house, hanging off the tree in the front garden, shouting and passing notes through the letter box, stopping and harassing anybody who tried to enter or leave. Young Gerald even took the hose to them from the bathroom window and they called the police. I told them, 'Well, get them off my property then,' but the police explained that they could stand on the pavement, which is about fifteen feet from my front door.

No matter what time of day or night you left the house they were there, cameras in your face and asking questions. One morning, towards the end of it, there was just one guy camping out there. When Gerald and a couple of his mates turned up at two in the morning they asked, 'Still here, mate?' Then said, 'Right, we're going to give you three minutes and then you're gone.' You couldn't see that feller's heels for dust.

One day the *Mirror* published a photo on its front page of Georgie in a trilby hat set to one side. I burst out crying; he looked so like my dad. I called my sister Phyllis, because I knew her husband Robert bought the *Mirror* to do the crossword. She'd seen it as well, and felt so sorry for me when I said that I couldn't even get out of my front door. That afternoon she was with me, having dropped everything and travelled from Ireland. Apparently Robert had said to her, 'I know you're only going to sit here worrying, so go over and see her.'

What the press refused to take on board was that somebody who is on drugs at that level is ill; don't tell me anyone in their right mind would stay in that state. Addiction is an illness, pure and simple, but the press turned George's into a media spectacle. At one time his manager Tony Gordon organised for us to move to a secluded farmhouse in West Clandon, Surrey in an attempt to get the family together away from the media gaze. They still got through, and I was approached so many times by journalists offering blank cheques to tell my story.

'What would possess me to say anything about my child?' I asked them. 'What's wrong with you people?'

'It must be heartbreaking for you,' one said.

'Yes, it is. And lots of mothers go through heartbreak but they wouldn't sell their children down the river.'

The press attention was amazing, and of course it had an effect on the rest of the family as well. It was tough when Kevin was charged with being one of George's dealers, while another of my sons, Gerald, also developed a taste for cocaine, which to me was unbelievable. Gerald had always been so athletic and proud of his sporting prowess.

When confronted with all that attention I had to

say to myself, 'Hold up. This is not my world; this is not the way we live.' I needn't have kept my job but I stayed there for twenty years because I loved it. It was mine. I had fought for that independence from my husband for so long. Down the years he had always been on at me to give up work, but I knew that would give him control of the purse strings. Having my own job and my own source of income represented independence from Gerald, and that's why he never liked it. I wasn't going to let even George's fame take my independence away from me.

I tried to ensure that my children had the same attitude, and I think maybe that's what got Georgie through the worst of these times. As we all know, he conquered his addiction and came to terms with the break-up with Jon Moss and went on to make a name for himself as a solo singer and DJ.

People I meet for the first time still ask, 'What's he really like?'

I really don't understand what they mean and always say, 'He's me son, love. He's like your brother. He picks his nose, he farts, does stupid things, wears socks with holes in them, just like anybody else.' The difference is that he can sing brilliantly and write great songs. When he's with me he's just my son. None of us say, 'Oh, Boy George . . .'

I've always maintained that attitude because it's natural to me. I remember when a friend invited me onto a local pub darts team. As soon as I got there I said, 'Youse all know who I am, but here I'm just

Dinah, one of the girls. I don't want to be treated any different to anybody else, and don't want anybody asking questions about him.'

And it worked out fine. I'm still playing darts, and to the girls I play with now I'm just Dinah. We have a great bit of fun. Sometimes I get tired and say I might give it up and they say, 'No, don't do that. Who'll make us laugh like you? Who'll crack the whip?'

Chapter Fifteen

I'll Burst Your Bubble

A night out with the girls from darts, early 90s

In 1986, at the height of Georgie's illness, we had use of the farmhouse in West Clandon, and in August that year my sister Teresa came to stay for a few days with her son Trevor and daughter Vanessa. It was a very stressful time but good to have my family around me, especially since Gerald was acting up and throwing tantrums as though it was him with the drug problem, not George.

One night after dinner, around midnight, Teresa and I were discussing Georgie's addiction when this almighty row broke out with Gerald. Teresa, who was very close to George and had ferried him all over the West Midlands when he lived up there for six months in the 1970s, was talking about how George could be very obstinate. She wasn't criticising him, but pointing out one of his characteristics.

I don't know why but this set Gerald off. 'How dare you?' he roared, banging the table. 'You don't even know my son! You're only here because he's famous!'

Vanessa ran frightened from the room, but little Trevor went over and put his arm around Teresa and said, 'Don't hurt my mam.'

This stopped Gerald in his tracks. 'I wouldn't hurt her. Honestly, son,' he said.

'Yes, I know you won't,' said Trevor, as if to say, 'Not while I'm here you won't.'

With that Teresa announced, 'I'm going home. I'll go and sleep at the station till the first train comes. Call us a taxi would you, Dinah? I cannot stay in the same house as him.'

I begged her not to but she was determined. However, while we talked, Gerald nipped out of the room and locked all the doors. 'She won't be going anywhere tonight,' he announced triumphantly.

The next morning I persuaded Teresa to stay for a few more days, because I knew Gerald was all out to get rid of her and isolate me.

Georgie had been up in London, and returned with a photographer for a magazine shoot. He had a load of clothes and insisted that Trevor and Vanessa take part. The kids had a great time and the photos were lovely.

Among the clothes was a pile of cardigans. Kevin had picked them up from one of the producers of *Absolute Beginners;* they even had the logo of the film inside the collar. George gave one to Teresa for Trevor and we all thought nothing more of it.

We drove back to Shooters Hill later that day, and I had a new green sheet which I also gave to Teresa. She wrapped the cardigan in it and put it away in her case in the back room where she was staying. As she packed Gerald came in to get something he'd left in there.

That week was one of the worst of my life. The next day I discovered that my son Gerald had been taking cocaine. He had had a furious argument with Siobhan, which was most out of character. He had even grabbed her by the neck, which for him was extraordinary. Maybe I'd developed a sixth sense from being around George, but I ordered him upstairs to his bedroom, sat him down and said, 'OK, I'm going to ask you a question. Don't lie to me. I can't help you if you lie. Are you taking anything?'

He nodded his head. 'Cocaine.'

I burst into tears in disbelief. Why was this fit, healthy, athletic young man doing this to himself?

Gerald was racked with shame and apologised profusely. As it turned out, he didn't use drugs for very long, but like Georgie he took everything – apart from heroin. I don't think they helped the balance of his mind one bit.

I told Gerald about my conversation with our son. He didn't help one bit but went mad, calling him names. 'You fuckin' idiot!' he yelled.

We had to leave that day to go back to Clandon, and the next morning Teresa came into the bedroom and said, 'Dinah, somebody's been found dead in Georgie's house in Hampstead.'

My stomach hit the ground. I was convinced that it was George, but within two minutes George was on the phone himself from his mews place in St John's Wood. This was when his friend Michael Rudetsky's body was discovered.

Billy Button drove down and picked Gerald and me up, and Teresa and the kids went back to Birmingham. George, as I have already said, was in a terrible state. Michael Rudetsky's mother later brought a case against George, accusing him of murdering her son, and I even spoke to her to try and get her to see the reality of the situation.

It had been a dreadful week, and on the Saturday, which was beautiful and sunny, I decided I would take Gerald up to Marks & Spencer in the West End and buy him a dogtooth jacket he had been going on about. It seemed a good idea to do something joyful – just us, a husband and wife out shopping. We talked about having lunch and then maybe taking in a matinee performance of a show.

At Marks Gerald tried on the jacket, and it looked great. We decided to buy a pair of black trousers to go with it and took a stroll looking for a place to eat. As we were walking down the street we spied these lovely black brogues in the window of a shoe shop, so we went in. He tried them on, and I bought them for him as well.

We came out and I was holding his hand, which was a rare occurrence, but I felt on top of the world after the miseries of recent weeks. We chatted about this and that, and then he said, 'Oh, I've got something to tell you about your sister.'

The way he said it alarmed me. 'Which sister? Why, what's she done?' I asked.

He then tried to brush me off: 'Ah, nah, it doesn't matter.'

'You can't do that, Gerald,' I said. 'What do you want to say?'

So he sighed and said that it was about Teresa. 'She's stolen a Kansai cardigan of George's worth six hundred pounds,' he said. I don't know where he got the name Kansai from, but I guess he thought it was an expensive designer label.

'What, my Teresa?' I cried. 'How do you know?'

'I found it in her suitcase when she stayed with us,' he said. 'I saw how she shut the case real quick when I went in, so thought I should go back and check what was going on. I found it wrapped in a sheet and took it out.'

I think what annoyed me more than anything else was the fact that he'd had the audacity to go through my sister's belongings. 'Are you standing there telling me that you walked into that back bedroom, opened my sister's case and rummaged through it?' I shouted.

He tried to calm me: 'Oh forget it. Let's go and have our lunch.'

There was no way that was going to happen now. I told him I wanted to go home. I knew how his mind worked: 'You think you can be happy, girl? I'll burst your bubble.'

He tried talking to me on the train all the way home but I would have none of it. When we got home I demanded that he bring me the cardigan. He stalled for time by attempting to get Siobhan on his side, saying that he had talked to her about it. She was just going out and said, 'Daddy told me about it but this has got nothing to do with me. I'm off.'

He would not bring that cardigan down and so I wouldn't talk to him. It was a stand-off. Then David said, 'For God's sake, Dad, show her the bloody cardigan!'

First he brought me the green sheet she had supposedly wrapped the cardigan in. 'I gave that sheet to my sister,' I coolly informed him. 'It was a present because she really liked it.'

He looked a bit taken aback and then produced the cardy. Of course it was the one from the pile at the photo shoot at Clandon. It was acrylic, nothing like a designer-label piece of clothing.

'Some little child in India probably got ten pence for making that, and it's most likely worth two and six,' I said. 'See that label? It says "Absolute

Beginners". Nothing to do with 'Kansai', but the film. Georgie gave this to Teresa for Trevor.' I went absolutely ape shit and went to hit him with my handbag, which was always heavily laden. I was enraged.

'Look!' he shouted at David. 'She was gonna hit me!'

And at that, all the years of fear and pain started to fall away. All over a cardigan, I know, but I said to myself as he cowered, 'This is what I've been frightened of all my life?'

I smashed and smashed my handbag against the front-room window till it cracked. I could hear him whimpering to David, 'Look at her! She's going berserk! She's a nutter! Look what she's just done to the window!'

'Berserk?' I snarled at him. 'Berserk?! I'll give you berserk! Get out of my sight! Go 'way! What possessed you to even think that Teresa would steal from us?!'

I was so angry, I think if I could have put my hands on him I'd have killed him that day. Instead I gave it to him chapter and verse. He'd always been two-faced about Teresa because she was one of the few people who stood up to him. Teresa used to stay with us every Christmas, but he'd always be carping about her. I said, 'No matter what you have said or done to her, she's never been scared of you in the least. And that's why you came up with this lie about her.'

That evening when he tried to talk me round I

gave it to him straight: 'You know what? You have killed every last ounce of affection I've ever felt for you. I don't know what's wrong with you but you cannot stop yourself. I've tried everything. They say, "Kill him with kindness." So I tried that. "Make yourself look pretty so he'll show you more love." I tried that. "Look dowdy so he won't get jealous." I've done that. Nothing has pleased you through this entire marriage,' I said. 'I don't know why you married me in the first place because you never seem to have been happy. But from tonight I'm sleeping in the back room. I don't want anything else to do with you.'

He looked like he'd been hit by a ten-ton truck. And, because I was so angry, I added, 'As a matter of fact, I hate you.'

Of course I didn't mean that. It was just my fury talking. The next day I told him, 'I'm not sorry about what I said apart from hating you. I've never hated anyone in me life and I don't want to start now. I'm apologising to you, and if you don't want to accept it, that's up to you.'

I also rang my sister and asked her why she hadn't told me about the sheet and cardy missing from her case. 'I thought that maybe you didn't want me to have them,' she said. When I told her what Gerald had done she confided that she had thought as much. I apologised but she said she was fine about the cardigan, and in fact didn't want it anymore.

Two days later she rang me and told me that Gerald

had posted it to her. 'What have you done with it?' I asked her.

'I've thrown it in the dustbin,' she said and laughed.

I felt myself gaining strength, though when I told Georgie he said, 'You were always strong, Mam. You allowed yourself to be browbeaten. That was the problem.'

But the night before I had moved to the back bedroom. We never shared a bed again.

Chapter Sixteen

The Worm Has Turned

Look at the state of it! The back garden at Shooters Hill

At the very start of the 1980s, Gerald's company began work on converting a property for L & T in Dulwich, not far from us in south London.

It was a massive job, a huge house ripe for conversion with an original well in the garden. It needed a lot of work but was a beautiful property: lovely round windows and a spiral staircase, that sort of thing. But the way Gerald handled it soon guaranteed that it became a financial and legal mess, one which rumbled on for seven years.

When he first took a look at it, in December 1980, another builder had already been involved and been paid the majority of the budget to convert it into seven self-contained flats. But he had barely made a start, and, so we were told, as soon as he had received the money – around £80,000 – he'd upped sticks and left L & Q to it.

It was then that Gerald entered the scene. Even though he was warned there was only £17,000 left in the pot, he took the job on, the idiot, without a written contract. I begged him to get something in writing, but he assured me everything would be fine, that a handshake was good enough. 'I know what I'm about,' he shouted. 'Don't tell me what to do.'

One day he took me to look at the job. He was always like that; rather than go on his own he would force me to accompany him, even to work. He'd cajole me to travel miles to meet a contractor, and I'd sit there with him as he talked to a total stranger. It's one of the great ironies of his life: this man who had such a forceful personality would turn into a little boy if he knew he had to go somewhere on his own.

Anyway, when I got to Dulwich I saw that the budget was far too small to finish the job. And I told him so. Every room needed plastering and fixing up; the original window frames had to be put back in, and he didn't know for sure whether the roof had been done. 'They reckon it has,' he said. 'Look, don't worry. They've said they'll reimburse me for any expenditure over the £17,000.'

Work started in early winter 1980, and they managed to complete the three top flats before the

Christmas break. But when he and his workers returned after the holiday, the three flats were ruined, soaked from top to bottom. He'd taken L & Q at their word that the roof had been renewed, and never bothered checking it for himself. Of course, it hadn't been. In addition, the property had been left insecure, and sinks and other fittings had been stolen.

The job dragged on and on and on. Gerald tried to negotiate for more money for the budget, but there wasn't any forthcoming, so he upped his loans and was soon £20,000 in debt to the bank. Of a Friday night, it was nothing for five or six men I'd never met before to be sitting in my front room, waiting for him to come home with their wages. He'd phone. 'Are they there? Don't tell them it's me.'

I lied on a daily basis. People would ring up: 'Can I speak to Gerry?' and I'd tell them he wasn't home while he was sat right there in front of me. It stunned me that this man, who had me scared shitless, couldn't face people and tell them the truth. I just don't know what went on in his head. He'd go out at nine o'clock in the morning and come home at one or two o'clock. You'd ask, 'Where have you been?'

'Out.' That would be the answer.

I wonder if I'd have done that, what would have happened? He would have gone apeshit, calling me every name under the sun, accusing me of all sorts of behaviour. But of course I never did find out because I didn't behave like that towards him.

Eventually, the stress and anxiety overcame him,

and in 1983, as George's career went into overdrive, Gerald suffered a serious heart attack.

One afternoon David was going with a friend of his down to Woolwich Magistrates Court, and Gerald said he would go along as well. Apparently, this mate of David's had been in some trouble, and after the case was heard and he'd been fined, this copper nicked him again outside the courtroom.

Gerald decided to intervene. 'I'm not having that!' David told me he shouted at the policeman. 'You can't be grabbing him like that.'

'Listen, mister,' explained the copper. 'This has got nothing to do with you. Go outside. There is another offence he has to answer to.'

But Gerald refused to leave. The policeman took the feller off and then came back. Gerald was still there, despite David's pleas that they should leave. 'The court is closing, so out,' said the copper, with his hand on Gerald's shoulder.

'Don't you put your hands on me!' said Gerald as he was bundled out of the door.

He must have felt so humiliated, and when he got back home he ranted and screamed the house down, beetroot-red in the face. He was like a lunatic. 'If you don't stop him, David, he's going to blow a gasket,' I said, but it was no good. Eventually after a couple of hours his rage subsided.

The following morning after I got up he complained of indigestion, and spent the next few hours in bed. When I asked him how he felt he said he had a pain in his arm, so I forced him to come to the hospital with me. Richard drove us down and they put him on a machine. The doctor confirmed that he had had a heart attack while he was asleep. 'Is he going to be all right?' I asked.

'Well, all heart attacks do some damage. We'll have to keep an eye on him.'

While he was recovering in hospital, I had a meeting with L & Q, taking with me photographs of the job before and after. 'Now look at how much work has been done by my husband, who is now in a hospital because of this,' I said, showing them the photographs. 'You told him that the roof was new, and it wasn't. Somebody else got £80,000 for doing nothing and now youse are not going to pay my husband anything for all his hard work? If there is no money forthcoming, I will go to the press myself tomorrow and show what a scandal this is.'

Within two or three days a cheque arrived for £11,000. I told Gerald what had happened at the meeting and he seemed satisfied, but instead of making that money work for him by doing the final few bits and pieces needed at the Dulwich site, it all went down the betting shop.

Still deeply out of pocket, Gerald decided to threaten legal action. A meeting was held at the bank in Eltham High Street with representatives from L & Q. There was a brief discussion and they left the room. After a short while one of the bank executives came back in and said that they had reached a settlement: the bank was prepared to wipe out the £20,000 loan, and L & Q was offering Gerald £17,000 in recompense. They were also prepared to give him more work. The bloke left us to think about it.

Gerald asked me what I thought. I told him it was a good deal and he should accept it.

'No, no, no,' he started. 'They're definitely in the wrong and they know it. Why would they wipe out twenty grand and offer me that money? I'm going to refuse it.'

And so he did. The fool. I don't know whether this was an Asperger's trait emerging; I know that sufferers don't apply the same logic as the rest of us to situations, and certainly his refusal of the offer made no sense at all. As a result his company collapsed but the battle over that bloody house in Dulwich went on for another four draining years.

In 1984 I was in hospital for seven days after having a hysterectomy, and Gerald was also experiencing more health problems. That same year the hospital ran tests on his heart and discovered he had hardening of the arteries. They recommended a bypass operation, but the next week Georgie was flying us to New York to see Culture Club play at Madison Square Garden and we really didn't want to miss that. When we explained that we were going on Concorde, and that the journey wouldn't be hard going, the doctor agreed that we could go, with the proviso that as soon as we returned Gerald was booked into the hospital.

Gerald was absolutely terrified. I said to him, 'Look, it's natural to be scared. Just talk to the doctor about it. And I'll be there from the minute you go in till the minute you come out.'

The doctor reassured him and the operation was a success. My friend Wilma, who was a nurse, told me what to expect when he came out of the theatre – that he'd be wrapped in silver material to maintain his body temperature, with tubes everywhere.

It was scary, I have to admit. I stayed with him all night, giving him water and making sure he was OK when he came round. Despite all he had put me through, despite the rages, the moodiness and the rapid-change personality shifts, I have to admit I still loved him, even at that late stage, and was very worried about his condition. By the next day they had him sitting up in bed chatting. He obeyed their instructions and knocked the cigarettes on the head. He didn't touch another one for eleven years, but then in the mid-1990s took it up again.

I think the whole experience knocked him for six, and he walked on eggshells for the next two years. During and after his recuperation he just didn't know what to do with himself. 'I can't go back to work,' he'd complain. 'I've just had a quadruple bypass!' In fact he'd had a triple bypass and I knew plenty of other people who'd been through similar experiences and had gone back to work after six months. Indeed I met an old boy at a bus stop around that time and he'd had two bypass operations. He was in his eighties and was as active as any man half his age.

I told Gerald he should find himself something to do, maybe work in a charity shop or at the hospital.

'What?' came the response. 'Work and not get paid for it? I don't think so!'

It was around this time that the compulsive side of his nature really came to the fore. He became a hoarder, like a magpie. Bad enough that he had built a huge, stinking pigeon loft down one side of the garden which he left to me to clean out, but behind that he had a shed, and another in the opposite corner, both of which he filled with total and utter rubbish. Not lawnmowers and gardening tools like a normal person, but anything abandoned and useless. He would never throw anything away: old toasters, kettles, battered old pots, bric-a-brac, building materials, paint, electrical bits and pieces, car parts, everything.

I remember once one of my chopping boards developed a split down the middle, so I threw it out. When I next went to the bins, it had gone; he'd retrieved it and added it to his mountain of crap.

'Somebody might have a use for it,' he protested when I challenged him. 'But it's unusable; the crack is harbouring germs. That's why I threw it out,' I said.

'Well I'll keep it and put it on the next bonfire.'

You just couldn't best him.

Soon he started on the house. The back room filled with hundreds and hundreds of carrier bags. The feeling I had was that he was pushing me to the limit, seeing how far he could go before I exploded.

There was a TV programme once about a little old man who had died, and the authorities couldn't get into his house for the rubbish he had collected. I told him, 'That's what's going to happen here if we don't watch out. And there's no way I'm allowing that in this house.'

I tried to talk to him, but to no avail. I worked with elderly people for twenty years, and would say to him, 'If only you could see what happens when people die. All their treasured possessions, all the stuff they have accumulated, is thrown in bags and then thrown on the scrap heap. Why don't we make a start on clearing up?'

But he was determined. 'It's all mine,' he would say. 'Just you leave it alone.'

He locked the back room. These days it is nice and light, looking out as it does onto the kitchen and garden, but back then only he had the key and was allowed in, filling it to the brim. After that room became chock-a-block, he filled the loft with junk and then fixed a lock on that.

What was it all about, this obsessive squirrelling away of all manner of stuff? And then the way it was locked away from us?

As the 1980s wore on his habits became more and more strange. At Christmas he wouldn't open any of his presents – apart from the one from George – but took them all, still wrapped, and locked them in the attic. I think the reason he opened George's was that he knew where he stood with him. George would tell him straight.

He had always been peculiar about presents. My brother Frank bought him a lovely lighter when we'd only been married five or six years, but that never left the box it came in. He put it away, never to be seen again.

One Christmas, after he had been going on about needing a new watch, I bought him an expensive one for his present. When I gave it to him he said, 'Oh, I haven't bought you anything, you know.' That didn't matter to me, but anyway he told me that it was a little bit loose on his wrist so I took it back and had some links taken out and gave it back to him. He never, ever wore that watch. It wasn't that I felt hurt; I just couldn't understand what went through his head.

As time wore on Gerald started on at me about stopping work, but I was adamant. 'I've given up one job for you and don't see why I should again,' I said. 'I enjoy what I do and I like the people I work with.'

His retort: 'Well, I shouldn't expect any sympathy from you.'

It was pathetic. But by now I was sick and tired of giving him money for the betting shop. I'd worked bloody hard all my life trying to make a decent home, and I wasn't going to have his gambling wreck it.

As the L & Q case ground on I became desperate to find a way of reaching a settlement, to get Gerald off my back and back to some kind of employment or at least something to occupy him. One day I heard a radio report about backhanders and overpayments regarding building work for the old GLC. They also gave out a telephone number for any aggrieved parties or those with information. I told Gerald about it and he called and arranged an appointment, taking in the boxes and boxes of paperwork he had amassed.

A solicitor agreed to take the case on a no-win, no-fee basis, but in fact Georgie eventually funded it to the tune of £15,000. He also gave his dad another £5,000 to get his company trading again and paid accountants £3,000 to carry out an audit and another £3,000 to a handwriting expert. The case was an obsession for Gerald, but it was always me who had to ask Georgie for the money. Meanwhile Gerald would be forever on about George's success: 'He's a millionaire. He could do anything he wants. He could buy houses and I could do them up.'

'That's his money,' I would say. 'We never helped him to get where he has, so he owes us nothing.' That's the one thing I am most proud of George – he did it all by himself.

By 1986 George's drug problems had become very serious, and I felt that I couldn't keep asking him for money. The problem was Georgie was so out of his head he didn't know what he was doing or what he was signing most of the time. I felt the pressure building. Gerald refused to drop the case, but insisted that I go with him to see the accountants, the banks, the solicitors, everybody. The press were everywhere and I felt utterly worn down by it.

Every night I'd have to sit and listen to Quadrant, Quadrant, Quadrant. We'd go to bed (I was still sleeping in the same room as him at the time) and it would be the same, sometimes until five o'clock in the morning. 'Please Gerald, can you just go to sleep?' I'd beg. 'I've got to go to work in the morning.'

'All right, I'm sorry,' he'd say. 'But I just wanted to tell you one thing . . .' And he'd go over the same ground, again and again. It was sheer torture, and this may seem strange, but I did feel sorry for him. He'd built up his own business which was now being wiped from under him.

When the case looked as though it was going to court, the bank held a meeting at our house in Eltham and demanded that I sign my insurance policies over to keep the funding coming. I refused, even though it would raise another £5,000.

Gerald ranted and raved at me. 'I have to have it!' he screamed. 'Don't you see, you silly cow, that this will save my skin?!' His octaves went higher and higher, the doors were slammed harder and harder and the threats started up again. It was like going back to the beginning, when he used to really lose it as a young man.

I said to myself, 'Oh my God, I don't want to go back to the way it was.' I wanted to feel safe. I couldn't see a way forward. But then I had an idea. It makes me ashamed to write this, and I'm crying now as I do, but suddenly I knew how to get round this without jeopardising the insurance. I decided the only way out was to write a cheque for that £5,000 and forge Georgie's signature. The way I looked at it, he wouldn't know, and the insurance policies would be protected. I feel desperately guilty to this day about that act because I betrayed my son.

It wasn't long before George's manager Tony Gordon picked up on it and challenged me. Of course I owned up and went straight to George and said, 'I'm really sorry. Your father needed the money and I didn't know what else to do.'

Georgie said, 'Don't worry, Mum; it's no big deal. But if you want anything, just ask me. And the next time he wants something, let him ask me himself. I don't know why you're still fetching and carrying for him.'

George had a point, that much was clear. I myself didn't know why I continued to be at Gerald's beck and call. Was it love? Duty? I found it so hard to relinquish my vows to honour and obey, in spite of everything.

Chapter Seventeen

Do What You Like

In Brighton with the girls from work, mid 90s

As time went on I got bolder. One day in the early 1990s during a coffee break at work the other girls announced they were going to Benidorm for a week. 'Oh gee, that would be great. I'll go,' I said. I rang my sister Phyllis and spoke to my friend Heather and they both said they'd come as well. I think there were about a dozen of us going, but I explained that I'd have to ask my husband first.

'What do you mean?' they all asked, apart from Phyllis and Heather who knew how things were. I'd never been anywhere without him before. 'You're fifty-two years of age, Dinah,' they said. 'Who cares what your old man thinks?'

When I talked to him about it, he just scowled and grunted, 'I can't stop you, can I?'

I told him that I wanted his agreement so that it would all be on a good footing.

'Why are they all going to Benidorm anyway?' he snapped.

'Just for a bit of fun,' I said.

'Ah, do what you like.'

All the kids urged me to go and Georgie gave me some spending money. Come the day of departure I asked Gerald to drop me down to where the coach was going to take us to the airport and he stopped me dead in my tracks. 'I can't,' he said. 'I've an appointment at the hospital. They think it's cancer.' He let the penny drop and then said airily, 'But it's nothing to worry about.'

Now of course I knew all about the boy that cried wolf through my long years with him, but thought, 'What if he's finally telling the truth?'

Young Gerald said to me, 'Mam, there's nothing wrong with him. Get in the car and I'll take you myself.'

Anyway he had achieved what he wanted, and really rattled me. I met up with the girls and when we got to the hotel in Benidorm, the first thing I did was look up at the roof. 'What are you up to?' asked one of them.

'Well, I just wanted to check. He might be up there, spying on me,' I said. That was the power this man still wielded over me.

It was great being with the girls because they dismissed my paranoia and we laughed from the beginning to the end of that week. By day we lay on the beach working on our tans and every night we'd go to this bar just across the road where this English guy did a great Tom Jones, with all of us on backing vocals. It was a bunch of silly women having a silly season, if you like, but it was fantastic.

When I came home I walked through the door and Gerald was sat in his chair. 'Oh you're back then, are you?' was the greeting from him. But the kids were excited to see me and that seemed to make it all worthwhile.

Phyllis went on back to Ireland, and all was well for a couple of days. Then, suddenly, I couldn't move. I don't know whether it was a delayed reaction to his attitude to my holiday, but my stomach was in knots, so painful I was immobilised.

I had some scans at the hospital and they decided to keep me in. 'What was she doing in Spain?' Gerald demanded of the doctors, as if they'd know.

'What's wrong with you then?' he badgered me. 'What did you get up to over there?' He kept on probing, increasing the tension I felt. But what had I done? Nothing. I had slept in the same room as my sister and my best friend. It had been totally inno-cent; none of us brought anybody back. But the more he kept on at me, the tighter my bowels were constricted.

They gave me all sorts of stuff, but I was totally

blocked up. Among the staff was this great big doctor who was very friendly. I called him Lurch, and he'd come and check on me every day, asking, 'Any movement today?'

Finally he prescribed me a laxative which he warned was incredibly potent. My only worry was that I'd have enough time to get to the toilet. So they administered it and when they left this old lady in the next bed said, 'God, I feel sorry for you. That stuff is dreadful.' But nothing happened, and Lurch had to give me two more doses before it had any effect. That was on my sixth or seventh day. By that time I was crippled with pain so they ran some tests to find out what was causing it.

Then Lurch came in and said, 'Well, Christina, downstairs seems to think you may have a growth, but I'm not so sure.'

He went to walk away and I called him back. 'Oy you, hold up. What are you talking about?'

Lurch said that the tests had been inconclusive as far as he was concerned, but it had been decided that I'd have an operation. During the operation they found no physical problem, but at a meeting with the consultant afterwards I was told that my condition was brought on by excessive tension. 'For some reason you are stressed out,' she said. 'You have to get to the root of it and try and rein in your anxiety because it's now having an impact on your health.'

It didn't take me any time to work out what was

at the root of my anxiety. I'd been inflicting this stress on myself by allowing him to get to me for decades. I knew it would be hard but I resolved to start working on myself and building up resistance to his manipulative ways.

Chapter Eighteen

Healer, Heal Thyself

Party for Siobhan's engagement to Craig, 1992

After I moved into the spare bedroom Gerald main-tained a constant barrage: 'You're breaking the marriage vows by not sleeping with me!' Or: 'So you're getting it somewhere else, are you? Is that it? Who is he? Tell me!'

It was typical of him. When he couldn't apply pressure one way, he would find another route to stress me out.

But I'd say, 'Where does it say in the wedding vows that you have to sleep with your husband? Show me. "For better and for worse, in sickness and in health"? I've done all that. "Till death us do part"? When I die we'll see about that, but until then, be quiet.'

And yet, however great my anger over his behaviour, I still loved Gerald, and believed that if he could only change his ways we would have a future together. I believed in the vows that we would have taken when we married, and wasn't prepared to give them up lightly, particularly since my faith was now so strong again.

It was ever so hard. Gerald became depressed and we entered yet another period where he became totally paranoid, convinced that the rest of his family was against him and that we were ostracising him. He said and did dreadful things. I remember coming home from work once and young Gerald was crying. I asked what was up and he said, 'I was having a chat with my mate Neil on the phone. When I finished Dad started in on me: "You were talking about me weren't you? What were you saying?" When I tried to tell him the truth he hit me over the back with a chair!'

One night, after a particularly bad row with young Gerald in which we all got involved he ran out of the house and stood at the top of the hill bellowing, 'The people in this house *hate* me! They're trying to get rid of me! They want me out!' It was insanity.

He'd done that before. I'd been staying with George in the late 1980s and had got back home late one night. The next morning I came down the stairs and remarked to Siobhan, 'The hall's very dark.' She just gave me a resigned shrug and led me out the front door. Above it over the glass he'd erected a cardboard sign on which he'd scrawled, 'The people in this house are bastards. They want me out.' Eventually we persuaded him to take it down.

As well as the downstairs back room and the loft, Gerald also fixed a lock on his bedroom door. I got in there one day and was rocked back on my heels by what I saw. Once again the room was full to the brim with carrier bags. He had even emptied his wardrobe of clothes – putting them on a shelf – so he could store more carrier bags there.

If he went to the post office, Gerald would take ten of each of the leaflets and pamphlets on display and bring them home. They wouldn't be used but stuffed into drawers. You'd ask him, 'What do you want these for?' and he'd snap, 'Just leave them there! They're mine. All right?' If I kept on and complained, he would take them out, put them in a plastic bag and tie it up and then stow it in the back room.

At one stage Gerald took to visiting members of my family when he went on trips to Ireland. He saw my brothers Frank and John and Frank's daughter Margaret, but my sister Phyllis told him to take a running jump.

When he came back he'd say the most horrible things, saying he'd met people in Dublin who were gossiping about my life there before I knew him. He said he'd met one of my nephews in a pub. 'He told me all about you and how wild you were.' He leered. 'I know all about you now.'

That man would only have been five or six when

I left Ireland, so couldn't have known anything about me. It was obviously fabricated.

Then he tried to stir things up between me and my sister's friend Norma, a quiet, gentle girl who he said had viciously attacked me for some of the quotes George attributed to me in his book *Take It Like a Man*. I didn't believe it anyway, but Norma confirmed his lies by saying, 'Dinah, I'm frightened of me own shadow. I wouldn't have the audacity to say such a thing.'

I couldn't believe how cruel he had become, trying to make up tittle-tattle. My son Gerald is convinced that his father was mentally ill, and certainly his behaviour tipped in that direction. He would totally condemn a person, and then turn up at their funeral and talk about them as if they were a saint.

Over the next few years George encouraged Gerald and me to try counselling, going to seminars at this place called Turning Point with him. They had helped him overcome his addiction and he accompanied us on the courses to help us sort out the issues that were thrown up. In truth I only undertook the counselling because of the benefit Gerald might gain from it. I knew where our problems lay, but he had to find out and understand them for himself before we could make any headway.

During one programme called Point of Choice you had to dress up as somebody you wouldn't normally be associated with. I dressed as an African queen, in a great big turban and a kaftan of George's encrusted with beads, and Georgie had black robes on and a Muslim-style face covering in brilliant gold. Then in Gerry walked with a mat on his front and a mat on his back.

'What is that about?' I whispered to Georgie.

'He's come as a doormat, Mum,' he said.

'Well that's something he's never ever been in his life,' I exclaimed.

During our time at Turning Point, Gerald mixed with others on the courses who were into healing, numerology, all that business. That world, and in particular reiki, became his new obsession. He took courses in reiki in London and qualified after just six months of study. How could he possibly have mastered the subject in that time? I worked with a woman who was still a novice after seven years. I have reflexology regularly and the people who treat me take years to understand their subject, so, I'm sorry, but I poured scorn on him when he turned up with his certificate after such a short time. I think he saw it as a money-spinning thing. He might have done well, he was so plausible. He could charm the birds off the trees. Some of my mates who didn't really know him would tell me, 'God, he's lovely isn't he? A real scream.'

'You want to live with him,' I'd say.

Anyway, I'm sure his charm helped him through all the tests they set him. When he proudly walked in with the pass certificate and a badge saying he could practise, I said to him, 'Healer, heal thyself.'

'Well, I wouldn't expect any praise from you,' he shouted. 'I've always had a talent for healing.'

It would have been funny if it wasn't so pathetic. I asked him who he had healed in the past.

'Bruce,' he said. That was his dog. He had removed something jagged from his paw, pure and simple.

'OK,' I said. 'And who else?'

'Well there was a duck once with a hole in its neck, and I helped it to recover.'

'So,' I said. 'That's a dog and a duck. But what about the dog you brought home you didn't care about? What about all those poor pigeons you left to rot in that loft?'

Of course he had no answer, just bluster.

Anyway, he set himself up in the then tidy back room with about twenty certificates on the wall proclaiming himself a reiki master. This was convenient, him attempting to heal other people, because that took the spotlight off him addressing his own problems. In fact, he was ranting and raving just as much behind closed doors, shouting the odds about everything under the sun.

Just before *Take It Like a Man* came out, Gerald went ape shit. 'I'll sue him!' he screamed. 'I'm not having my life displayed for everyone to read! I'll take him to court!'

I tried to calm him: 'For Chrissake, Gerald! If he's going to tell the truth, it can't hurt you. I don't know what he's going to say about me, but I'm not worried.'

Having said that, when I first looked at it, I said

to myself, 'I can't read this book.' There were details of his sexual life which no mother should be party to. I had to put it down. Siobhan didn't read it for a couple of years. She said, 'He's my brother; I don't want to know about that.'

I spoke to my sisters and none of them had read their copies either. But then George asked me to so I sat and read it over two or three nights. I found it, and his second book *Straight*, very, very honest. I liked it and was surprised at the amount of people who come up to me and asked me to sign copies.

One woman, Ena, came from Wellington Street like me, and asked me to get him to sign it. 'It's brilliant. Tell you what though,' she said. 'He's too bloody honest for his own good!'

With Gerald, I was increasingly finding my voice, and this made him scream and shout at me all the more, because I wasn't prepared to accept his nonsense or his secrecy.

I was determined to remove the lock he had placed on our loft, and one day I got Kevin to take the lock off and open the trap door. Inside was the usual junk he accumulated. I deliberately left the loft door open for him to see, and he went mental. But this time I was determined and ordered lorries from the council to take it all away. It took five of them to remove it all from the garden sheds, the back room and the garden. It cost me five hundred pounds, but it was well spent.

He became terribly spiteful around this time and would put me down more than ever. One night we were discussing the operations we'd had, and he totally forgot I'd had a hysterectomy. He was that self-obsessed that when I mentioned it, he snapped, 'What operation? I don't remember that.' Every conversation with him would quickly descend into him talking about himself. It was all 'me', 'my' and 'I'. I was so patient with him, I realise that now.

But of course his new friends never saw any of that.

One day he brought home two old ladies who had travelled all the way from Wales to take part in his Reiki course. One sat with me at the kitchen table while he talked to the other in the front room. 'God, your husband is ever so good,' said this woman. 'He did a fantastic reading for my friend over the phone. Are you also a healer?'

'No, I'm not,' I told her.

She asked me whether I believed in it, and I said, 'I can't say whether I do or I don't but I know there are people who get a lot from it.' What I really wanted to tell her was: 'If you only knew. Not just what he was like before he started on this, but even now, when he's shouting and screaming and putting us all down.'

I really think he started to lose it around this point. Whatever young Gerald took up, he would follow. His son started a strict fitness programme and passed with flying colours, so he had to take part as well, but failed. 'That's because she didn't like me,' he said of the trainer. 'She's a lesbian.' Nevertheless, he was determined, and took the course again and passed.

He had always needed to be in control but as the kids grew up they found their own feet and challenged him, particularly Georgie and Siobhan. She was never going to let anybody treat her the way he treated me. When they rowed, and he became so enraged he raised his fist, she would say to him, 'Hit a woman, would you? What kind of man are you?' I don't know whether it was because she was living with us or because she was a woman he couldn't control, but she bore the brunt of his behaviour during this period

One evening they had a massive row, and the next day her jewellery box went missing from her room. We were all out of the house apart from him, and he came up with a story that we had been burgled. The police were called but the only thing missing was the box. I could never pin it on him or persuade him to admit to it, but I seriously believe that he lost control after the argument and decided to wreak his revenge by stealing that box. Certainly one of the coppers who visited us said that it all seemed very strange, and tipped me the wink that he didn't believe Gerald's story in the least.

In 1995 we as a family faced the darkest period in all of our lives when my son Gerald was arrested over the death of his wife Gill. It was a terrible time; she was such a lovely girl. George came and stayed to help fend off the media.

I was in a desperate state when the news broke. But the one person I needed comfort from – my husband – couldn't be bothered. He was staying with relations in Bristol, and when I phoned him, he sighed and said, 'Oh no. I can't cope with this! I can't take anymore!' It was typical of his self-centred nature to turn it on himself rather than think about what his son was going through. I put the phone down.

Initially, Gerald spent a few weeks at a prison in Milton Keynes, and I visited every day. Later he was moved to a hospital in Enfield, and again I visited him every day. If Gerald ever came with me, he would lose his way. It's a fairly straightforward journey from north to south and Siobhan wrote the route down for him, but he'd get lost and we'd be an hour late and it would cause no end of problems so eventually I put a stop to him driving me there.

In my heart I knew that young Gerald hadn't meant to do it. My priest visited him when he was in hospital and took confession. I know that they are not allowed to divulge what is said, but I was consoled when Father Hooley said to me afterwards, 'Don't worry. You are right in what you're thinking.'

As a family the whole dreadful story brought us closer together than ever. These days young Gerald lives in a flat close to the rest of us in south London, and he has all our love and support, as we know we have his.

He is studying for a degree now, becoming more confident and is much more able to communicate.

I've asked him to write down all of the significant experiences in his life, even if he is the only person who reads it. I think he needs to understand his life, and setting it down would be beneficial. I don't think he has come to terms with what he did, and I don't think he ever will. The hardest thing he had to do was meet Gill's mother a few years ago. He was so scared when we sat and talked about it, but he agreed he had to do it and got through it.

I have been in contact with Gill's mum on a regular basis and always send a Christmas card. It is still also very tough for Gerald, and I feel for my son every day.

Chapter Nineteen

He Couldn't Even be My Friend

Gerald and Siobhan on her wedding day, July 1995

With the kids all moved out Gerald and I started to live separate lives, though I always held out hope we could sort out our differences. He continued to scream and shout at every opportunity, but at the same time he got more and more into reiki, spending a lot of time away, apparently on courses in healing therapy.

One night he brought a fellow student to stay; she had missed her train home, across London to Enfield. I gave her supper and made a bed up in the spare downstairs room he had taken over as his own.

Not long afterwards, in January 1999, Georgie threw a party at his house in Hampstead for my sixtieth birthday and Gerald's sixty-fifth. The female friend was present again as Gerald's guest. I didn't notice anything myself, until I saw her sat on one of those ornate chairs of George's. I waved at her, but she returned my gesture with a piercing glance. She looked absolute daggers at me. I said to my sister, 'What's the matter with her? Silly cow,' and thought no more of it. But some of my kids were disgusted that she should be present on such an occasion, and challenged him about the nature of their friendship. George even asked him if he was having an affair. He insisted their relationship was platonic, nothing more.

A few months later it all came out. George paid for a holiday in Ireland for his father; that was his usual birthday present to us both – a nice trip abroad for Christmas and then spending money on our birthdays. The travel agent called to check something in the booking with Siobhan, who always looks after things like that for George, and as she was going through the details she discovered that there was a ticket in the name of the same woman who had stayed under my roof and visited George's house. They'd also booked a cottage for themselves.

Siobhan didn't tell me immediately; she wanted to talk to the others about it. But I discovered for myself the very next day when I came across a guide to cottages in Ireland in the kitchen. Inside was a letter to a woman named Sarah at an address in Enfield. That was typical of Gerald; he could never face the truth, so left it for me to find.

I didn't even confront Gerald that day, but

nevertheless all hell was let loose because he knew what was coming and started an almighty argument so that he could storm out. He went berserk, threatening to kill me, to burn the house down, shouting about killing me and everybody else in the area, threatening 'another Dunblane massacre'.

I was so frightened I called the police for the first time in my life. No matter what violence or cruelty he had subjected me to in the past, I had never resorted to that. After that he knew it was over, that he couldn't frighten me anymore.

As I was asking the police to come over, Gerald walked past me and muttered, 'You can't prove nothing.' It transpired that the policewoman at the end of the line heard him. They later visited him, though I will never know what they said to him, but afterwards he said, 'It doesn't matter anyway. I'm a nutter.'

'What does that mean, Gerald?' I asked him. 'Why are you doing this? If you want to go, just walk out the door; just say you want to go.'

'What d'ya mean?' he sneered. 'You can't put me out. Half this house is mine.'

At that, something clicked. I realised that his frustrations and rages were no longer to do with me or even his children, but money. Pure and simple. He had decided to go but didn't want to lose out on the half share of the house he thought he was due. This nutter act was all to get me to agree to a split and the sale of the property, which George had bought from the council a couple of years earlier so that I would always have a place to live.

'I know exactly what your game is, Gerald,' I told him. 'You're going to try and have the house sold. Well I'm sorry – over my dead body.'

His whole demeanour changed. 'Try and stop me,' he said coolly.

The police arrived and recorded the incident, but now I was on my guard.

The next day I talked to Siobhan about the letter, the row and the threats, but didn't know what to do. At that moment Gerald came down the stairs. 'How dare you threaten my mother?' Siobhan shouted at him.

'Ah she gets on my nerves,' he snarled. 'I'm going.'

So off he went, to stay with Sarah until their holiday started a few days later, and Siobhan told me about the conversation she had had with the travel agent and everything fell into place. I felt a mix of emotions.

This was somebody who had railed against me for 'breaking our marriage vows' because I wouldn't sleep with him, yet he was perfectly happy to go behind my back and cover his affair up with all sorts of subterfuges. It would have been right and proper for him to have come to me and said, 'Look, this is not working,' instead of lying about going away on numerology courses for the weekend, that sort of thing.

Maybe it was the honesty and openness that I learnt from my father, but I had no idea what had been going on. I've never been a jealous person. Envy has never played a part in my life, so I naturally assumed she was his friend, nothing more.

Later, I learnt that a friend of hers had once said to Georgie, 'Isn't it wonderful that your father's found love?' That brought me a lot of pain. Those people knew nothing about me – who I am, how much and how often I got nothing in return for the love I showed that man. I was also angry that Gerald had dragged other people into his lie, and abused his son's generosity in that way. If George had known he was paying for her as well, he would never have given Gerald the holiday.

Her father repaid Siobhan for uncovering his deception at her wedding the following year. Warning her beforehand, 'This is one day you can't shut me up,' he became outrageously drunk at the reception and peppered his speech with lines like 'I am sooo *fucking* proud of my *fucking* daughter . . .' Eventually, he was silenced by the toastmaster. All of us – family and guests – were stunned with embarrassment at the show he made of himself.

In 2001 our divorce became final after forty-two years of marriage. A friend of Gerald's later told me that he said he put in for the divorce just to see what my reaction would be, but by that time I think I'd been insulted enough. I then received a letter from Gerald's solicitor trying to force the sale of the house. Even though George had bought the property, the deeds were in both our names.

I told George, 'I'll go home or live with one of my family. Sell it now and let's be done with it.'

Gerald asked to be bought out for £70,000, and because George knows how much I love my house he paid him the money. After that Gerald stopped communicating with George; never phoned him. I don't know that Georgie even received a thank you.

They never spoke again. George would have given him money if Gerald had said openly, 'Listen, son, I don't want to stay with your mam and I'm moving out. Can you help me with a property?' But he chose to go about things in a way which would have literally left me without a home.

A son and a father should not be estranged, so that became a source of sadness to me, but I know George did the right thing.

His second wife has recently said in the press that Gerald tried to make up with George but that's not true. George would have welcomed contact, but the first move had to come from Gerald because George was so hurt by what he had done. After Gerald walked out he maintained contact with David and young Gerald, but he never even rang me. Both of them wanted to continue to see their dad, and that's fair enough because all of my children wanted him to be proud of them.

But young Gerald believed that contact had to be based on the truth, and unfortunately that wasn't forthcoming. Once when his father visited Gerald, he asked him about the time he had pulled a knife on me when young Gerald was fourteen, he apparently said, 'No, Gerald, it wasn't like that at all. Your mother came at me with a broken bottle.' Maybe it was his justification in front of his new wife.

Gerald said, 'Dad, I was there! I told you to get out of the house!'

So apparently his father said to his wife, 'Right. Come on then; let's go!'

The cruellest thing was that, before they left, she said to Gerald, 'You know your father said he took the flak for you?' To claim that he had suffered for what young Gerald did was not only devastating, it was untrue.

In 2002 my lifetime of smoking caught up with me, and I was hospitalised with emphysema. The kids rallied round and George was particularly upset. He stayed at the hospital for days and kept an all-night vigil at my bedside. While I was out of it, he was told by the medics that I might not make it through till morning. It was a desperate period. Yet during all my time in hospital Gerald only visited me once, and couldn't bring himself to even hold my hand as I lay there enfeebled – me, the woman who had borne him six children and stood by him through thick and thin.

He had married Sarah in 2001 but the children weren't invited. Not that they wanted to go anyway. A friend of Siobhan's called her and said that her brother had been asked to be best man. When Siobhan told her brother Gerald, he rang the old man. 'When were you going to tell your children?' he asked.

'Oh, did you want to come?' his father said breezily.

By all accounts they had a nice time together with her two children, going on holidays and living a good life. That's painful, if only for the effect it had on our own children. Here was somebody who had earned a lot of money at different stages of his life, yet we would go to Margate or places like that. To hear about his trips to Greece, Spain and Egypt with his new family was hurtful, not just for me, but for our kids. I can't fathom it.

Our first Christmas together as a family without him was very pleasant. There were no rows or upsets, or those huffs he used to throw, jumping up from the table and storming silently out, leaving us all feeling as though he'd been offended and we didn't know why. We had a happy day, but it was tinged with regret, because I wished he could have been there to see how easy it is to have a good time together without unnecessary friction. As I played with my grandchildren I thought to myself, 'Why isn't he here playing with them as well?'

When Siobhan's Molly was born in 2002 he visited, but he didn't see her youngest, Zak, until he was about two years old. Whatever the circumstances, I couldn't not see my grandchildren, so it was quite revealing that he seemed to be able to put our part of his life behind him so readily. If we spoke on the phone he would say how much he loved all his grandchildren, yet he never visited them and only went to David's house twice in six years.

One thing was very strange: in all the years he lived with me he never wrote a single birthday card, but as soon as he left he started sending them, not only to the kids but also to my sisters Teresa and Phyllis.

They'd have weird messages in them. Vanessa, my niece in Birmingham who has a boy with Down's syndrome, received one from him which said something about how when Gerald had spoken to her on the phone, he'd felt her presence with him, even though she wasn't there. That scared Vanessa a little bit. She sent it to me and asked, 'What does he mean?'

My sister Annie got one which went on about him still being part of my family even though he and I were no longer together. It seemed he could write things which he would never express to your face. At Easter 2004 he sent a twenty-pound cheque and cards to Siobhan's kids Molly and Zak, and put in the covering note to her, saying he'd always love her, and that he missed seeing her, but his love was with her everywhere. Those were words he never spoke to her in person. Siobhan never cashed the cheque.

Over the following years George made me so proud with his West End musical *Taboo*, some of which centred on his early life, with characters based on me and his father. I went to see it several times during its London run, and really loved the way Georgie depicted his life. The duet sung by the mother and son, 'Stranger in This World', was really heartbreaking. I went with my mate Heather and cried my eyes out.

> You always knew, didn't you, mother?
> You always knew, as mothers always do
> You always knew, didn't you, mother?
> I was a stranger in this world.

The character based on George's dad was also very true to life, and I know that Gerald went to see it, though I don't know what he thought.

The first time I saw it was at the read-through, with Matt Lucas as Leigh Bowery. I sat there thinking, 'This is Georgie's life story here, and that's me on that sewing machine.'

I said to him afterwards, 'That's your life, Georgie, isn't it?'

He was really funny. 'No, it's not, Mam. It's about the '80s, about the nightclub Taboo, blah, blah, blah.'

But I knew better. It was a very fair depiction, I thought, and the scene where Leigh Bowery dies is really affecting.

Taboo eventually transferred to Broadway in November 2003. All the family were flown over for the opening night, and I've never been prouder, sitting in the packed theatre in New York watching everyone gathered there for my son. Young Gerald and I took a bus tour around Manhattan, and in the theatre district I nudged him and said, 'Oh look, there's your brother.'

And there was this massive billboard towering over Times Square with Georgie's face on it, advertising *Taboo*. I got him to take a photo, and even though the billboard is tiny in the distance, I know it's him. A lady on the bus asked what we were doing. 'Taking a picture of my son,' I said. 'There he is. See him up there?'

'Oh gee, ohmigod . . .' And suddenly all the other ladies on the bus were crowding around.

I felt sorry that George's father couldn't find the dignity to come to America and join in what was really a celebration of our son's success. I also found it really sad that, when Gerald left, he couldn't even be my friend. After all our years together he couldn't take my hand and say, 'Look, I'm really sorry it didn't work out.'

The day he walked out of my life I felt such mixed emotion: glad that at last the boil had been lanced, but also great loss. Not only had I lost the kids' father, the presence that had been with me for such a long time, but I had also lost the battle to help him find some peace of mind.

I had tried so hard over the years, but now felt a failure; I would never get through to him. Don't get me wrong: I wasn't out to change him in any way. Inside him I believe there was a lovely person, but I could never reach it. I don't know why, but the realisation of that fact made me deeply sad. However much he had mistreated me, the simple things hurt me after he had gone, even the knowledge that he would never again sit at the table for a meal with me.

I also felt guilt that I had allowed him to get away with terrorising us with his rages for so long. What effect had that had on my children? I did my best, I know that, and I made our house a home. I worked hard, washing and scrubbing and making ends meet, but could I have done more to protect my kids from him? It's a question which has no answer for me.

Chapter Twenty

At Last He's at Peace

By the Trevi fountain, Rome, 2004

Quite early on the morning of 4 September 2004, Siobhan burst into my bedroom in tears. 'What's the matter, love?' I asked.

'Dad's dead,' she sobbed.

It was a total shock. You don't spend forty-odd years with somebody and handle news like that well. Gerald had been on holiday in Egypt with his second wife, out in a boat. Apparently, he'd been in the water, and after clambering back suffered a massive heart attack. He died instantly.

The very next morning his wife had called young Gerald, who had maintained contact with his dad, and he then rang our house.

Siobhan and I sat on the bed and wept together. I told her, 'He was your father and you loved him, however much you argued. I loved him as well, darling.'

Of course the thoughts came rushing in. What if? If only.

Soon the shock was replaced by a feeling of utter sadness that our marriage had ended like it did. Despite every effort I had made. In all our years together I had never been aggressive to him, always tried to find a way to calm him down. Then I felt anger that everything had been taken out of my hands. We would never be able to make it right between us. There was nothing we could do now.

Amid all the feelings which coursed through me on hearing the news, there was one which was absent: relief. Isn't that strange? After all he had put me through you would have thought that I might have sighed, 'At last, it's over.' But that didn't happen. Instead, I was distraught. After one particularly bad episode, Gerald had once asked me if I wished him dead. I said, 'No. I could never wish anybody dead.'

In the months after his death I did start to feel relief, not for myself but for him. I still feel immense sadness, but that is tempered by the knowledge that he is at peace. I believe he spent a lot of his life in torment, and thank God that is now at an end. I remember my Phyllis once said to me, 'You know what, Dinah? He is such a lucky man his kids love him the way they do.' But he could never see that, which is a great shame.

Talking about his death is still very emotional for me. When I lie down of a night I go over aspects of his life and our relationship in my head. Did I cause him to react in a particular way? Was it my fault? But then I know in my heart of hearts that I tried to help him, that I wasn't to blame. My faith has meant a lot to me and has helped me through.

Soon I learnt from my children that his wife was going to handle all the funeral arrangements. She was in communication with Gerald and David, and the info was then passed back to me. Because of the bureaucracy and red tape involved in a British national dying overseas, it cost a lot of money to bring him back. It was weeks before his body arrived in the country. The funeral didn't take place until well into October, more than a month later.

Aside from all the complications in bringing his body back home – never die abroad, that's my advice – a hoo-ha soon developed over the service.

We heard that his wish had been to be cremated and that the service shouldn't be Catholic. Twice the funeral was postponed, but then a date was set at their local C. of E. church in Enfield very close to where he lived with his new family.

I wanted to see him in his coffin, but his wife said that the instruction was that nobody could do that. She told one of the boys that we wouldn't want to see him anyway, because he was disfigured and discoloured, but that should have been our choice, and it was taken away from us. OK, I may have been shocked, but I wanted to see him, to get that closure, as they say, after all the years of turmoil and heartache.

I had lots of things to tell him, not least the know-ledge I had gained from reading the book about Asperger's, *Loving Mr Spock*. I also wanted to tell him about all the years I wrote down my prayers: 'Please God, help me to understand why he is so angry.'

During the service, a few people got up and talked about the man they knew. I didn't recognise the Gerald they spoke about at all. When one lady talked about 'Jeremiah' and how he liked to go to Harrods, I thought, 'Well, you didn't know him.' He never went to Harrods. My sister Teresa cried, and I tried to console her. Through her tears she wailed, 'I'm crying for *you*; these people don't know him!'

I couldn't understand the service at all: afterwards he was sent off from the church on his own. Nobody accompanied him to the crematorium, and this was a man who, throughout his life, hated his own company. Everywhere he went either I had to go, or one of the children, sitting outside the betting shop or with him on a job.

I was told that was his wish, but again that wasn't the man I knew. He must have reinvented himself when he walked out of my life. He'd been working up to that for a long time – following in young

Gerald's tracks when he studied to be a masseur, visiting a healing church in Charlton, passing all those reiki exams in a matter of months – but when he got together with Sarah the reinvention was complete. Then he could turn his back on the bad things he had inflicted on us all and say, 'Well, that never happened. Look at me now. Do I behave like the kind of person who would do that?'

After the funeral my family and friends came back to the house. I sent a hundred pounds down to the Chinese takeaway and the fifteen of us sat and ate Chinese and talked about the bizarre events of the day.

Now my heart is full; the anger and regret are subsiding. I don't wish away the years, but feel sorry for Gerald for burying his intelligence and potential under cascades of violence, envy and greed for so many years. His self-obsession knew no bounds. Spencer Bright, who co-wrote George's first book *Take It Like a Man*, spent a day interviewing him for background material and came away with seven hours of tapes. I spoke to Gerald later about it, and Spencer said, 'They were no good to me. He spent the entire time talking about himself.'

Unfortunately, that was Gerald's life: listen to me, look at me, I want this, this is mine. Me, myself, I. He had to have the lion's share of everything.

In Georgie's second book, *Straight*, which he completed after his dad died, he was able to be more honest about his father. Gerald got off very lightly in

Take It Like a Man, but I admired George's honesty in the face of his death.

Gerald remains an enigma to me and I admit to being fascinated still. I was scarred by him, and scared of him. It's now more than two years since he died and I have to say that I am only now coming to terms with it.

I realised when he died that I would never figure out where his anger came from. Even if he didn't hit you, he'd scare you so much with his fury you'd be in flitters. He'd slam one door and then another, walk out of the room and then storm back in, the octaves getting higher and higher until you were literally shaking in your shoes.

I asked his Aunt Kitty about it. She told me that even as a child he would kick and scream if he didn't get his way. I do believe that his own mother was scared of him. Remember I went to her when he beat me, when I was pregnant with George, and she said, 'I've told you before not to answer him back.'

Although I still ponder the true nature of his character, I revel in the freedom I have now. There was a time when I couldn't sleep, and too many nights that phrase nagged in my brain: 'Handsome bastard . . . handsome bastard . . . handsome bastard . . .'

I put a lot of what I took from Gerald down to the shame I felt over becoming pregnant by Seamus as a young girl. It's only in the last ten years that I've stopped feeling guilty, and I think I was so delighted when Gerald followed through on his promise to marry me I would have put up with anything. Which of course is what I did. My kids could never understand. 'What do you feel so guilty about?' they'd ask. Like the time when I told Siobhan that Richard wasn't her father's son. I sobbed, but she said, 'It's all right, Mum, it's no big deal. He's my brother.'

But all that's receded now. I'm getting over it, slowly but surely. I have reached equilibrium over the four decades I spent in the company of this strange and extraordinary individual.

He is silent now.

Afterword: I Made My Bed

So, when all's said and done, my father was right. I did make my bed and I did lie in it, for better and for worse. I don't regret a thing, because I came through it. I survived torments which pushed me to the limit but I have had and am still enjoying a great life, raising a family of brilliant kids. I am genuinely happy these days and have learnt from sometimes bitter experience, but I hope you understand by now that this is no sob story.

However timid I was as a child, and innocent as a young girl, I was determined not to be ground down. In many ways I was lucky, because I had the support system provided by my parents and brothers and sisters. That is certainly something lacking in this day and age. I watch programmes about unmarried mothers and teenage pregnancies and want to say to the young couples involved, 'If only you could stop and look at what you're doing to each other.' Some of these kids, not even twenty years of age, have three or four children and no support, raising them in desperate circumstances. Is it any wonder they turn on each other? But it's heartening to see that when the children get to a certain age some women have the opportunity to go back to school and study, or take control. Then, maybe, their lives haven't been in vain.

But the pressure on young women and girls is incredible. I was on a bus recently with young Gerald and three girls got on with make-up and lipstick and these tight, revealing clothes. They were about twelve years old and absolutely skinny, to the bone. One was telling the others that she has to watch what she eats all the time because she puts weight on. I thought, 'You're just babies.' Kids aren't allowed to enjoy their childhood anymore. I wanted to sit them down and give them a good talking to.

Also, if it's not already clear, I want to state that Georgie's fame is just another fact of our lives, and something we have long come to terms with. We all cope with the pressures that fame sometimes brings and bear the strain together, like when Georgie was arrested in New York in the early hours of one day in October 2005. The media ran all these stories about him being found with mountains of drugs on him when, in fact, he was let off with a caution and a fine for wasting police time.

It's only because I have had so much experience of the way the press distorts everything that I knew he would be OK, but I was very worried nevertheless when the call first came through to our house from George. He was being held at a police station and had called Siobhan so that she could organise a lawyer for him. All I could hear her saying was, 'Just be calm, George. Calm down, please.' He was beside himself, and who wouldn't be?

I lay there worrying. Would he keep his mouth shut and be polite? I know what I'm like, and wanted him to just keep to the routine: 'Yes, sir. No sir. Three bags full, sir.'

Siobhan called George's friend Amanda Ghost who arranged a lawyer so that George had legal representation by the time he was in court the next morning.

They were hell-bent on doing him for drugs. How they claimed that they saw drugs by his computer when they were only at the door I don't know. Siobhan knows that apartment and told me how his computer was in his office, obscured by two walls at the other end of his huge flat. He was compos mentis by the time they arrived, and apologised for having called them, but they went away and got a warrant on the basis that they had seen some drugs. When they returned they told him they were taking him downtown, even though he had apologised for calling them. I believe this was because of who he is. One thing I am very pleased about is that Georgie is now back living in London. He was in New York for two years, so it is great to have him back home these days.

George had to fly back and forth to New York three times before they handed down the judgment of a fine and five days' community service. He offered to perform a free concert or work in a hospice but they said no, and I am proud that he carried out the street-sweeping so whole-heartedly, though after the first day when we watched the press crawling all over him, Siobhan and I wanted to go out there and help immediately.

The New York sanitation department said he was one of the best workers they have had. Just like me he got on with the job and tried not to let the media get to him as they dragged all the stuff out about his illness from the 1980s, nearly twenty years before. That really aggravated me.

Back then we all knew that half the media were on the stuff themselves. I remember confronting one journalist: 'Why are you writing this about my son? You're on the same stuff yourself!'

He smiled smugly and said, 'Yeah, but I didn't get caught.'

Why do the media hound people who have an illness? I don't understand it. Alcoholics, drug addicts, gamblers say the same thing: 'The next drink, the next snort, the next bet is going to make it all right.' They are taken over by their addictions. But instead of trying to help these people, the press savages them.

I remember one particular tabloid journalist who treated George terribly. He turned up in our hotel in New York when *Taboo* was opening, all cheery. 'Hello, Mrs O'Dowd!'

'Don't you come near me!'

George said, 'Mam, don't worry. I don't care.'

'Oh come on, Mrs O'Dowd.'

'You stabbed my son in the back; I don't want to talk to you.'

He said, 'But that's years ago, all over and done with.'

I told him, 'It might be all over and done with for you but I have a great memory and I will never forget what you wrote. You were a drug addict as much as him, you hypocrite.'

I remember the time I met Princess Diana. After we chatted, a journalist came sidling over. 'What did you talk about?' he asked.

I said, 'It's a private conversation and nothing to do with you. I know all about you and your cocaine habit.'

During the run-up to his court case in New York in 2005, George's new management decided that the couple who operated his DJ business should be let go. It was time for them to move on. They had worked for George for two decades, travelling the world and enjoying all the luxuries that come with the business, but still they sold their story to the *Mail on Sunday* claiming that he was a cocaine addict and close to death.

The day before this story was published George had a show at London Fashion Week for his clothing label B-Rude. It was a fantastic event, where Georgie displayed his showmanship in a totally new field. He was picked especially to close the week, which made me very proud. All the family was there rooting for him, and one of Richard's sons, Jason, even modelled, walking down the catwalk in a B-Rude outfit.

After the show a woman who worked for the *Mail* sidled up to me. 'I wondered whether you would like to give me a quote,' she said.

'About what?' I asked, my suspicions rising to the surface. You develop antennae over the years.

'The fashion show,' she said.

I told her that I thought it had been fabulous, and I was pleasantly surprised at the designs my son and his co-designer and friend Mike Nicholls had come up with.

Then she switched. 'Well now, what about this thing in New York?'

But I'm not taken in that easily. 'Listen, love, that's got nothing to do with this, and I've got nothing to say about it.'

'Oh that's sweet,' she simpered. 'Do you think you could get me backstage so I could talk to George about it?' As if. I told her that nobody was allowed back there, winked at the security girl so she wouldn't be let through and left her to it.

The next day the *Mail* published a tiny bit about the B-Rude show and gave much more space to the story by George's former DJ employees. I thought it was diabolical. They may have fallen out with him at the end, but they earned money from him over twenty years, and he always gave them credit for their work, and paid them well. I don't know how they had the gall to do it.

In the same paper a few weeks later there was an outrageous story about my husband's memorial service, claiming that George shuffled into the church, head bent like a broken man, and begged everyone to pray for him – not his father – because of the New York case. What balderdash. Nothing of the sort occurred. The icing on the cake was a quote from Gerald's wife saying that she had bent over backwards to accommodate us for the funeral but that we hadn't invited her to the memorial service.

I don't know whether she said that or not, but if she did, she must be mad to think that I would invite her to a memorial service in a Catholic church. The final insult was that she wouldn't give the children his ashes. Maybe this was another one of his wishes but it doesn't seem fair and now all I have to remember him by is a little plaque on a bench in the grounds of St Thomas More in Eltham.

The irony of my life is that I came so close to cracking the enigma which was my husband, and then he left me and died. If I could have had one last chat and told him the information I had gathered on subjects such as Asperger's, I think it would have been of great help, both to him and me.

Two months before he left he asked me a curious question: 'All these things I'm supposed to have done to you? Do you remember them?'

'Yes,' I said. 'Every single thing. Whenever you shout at me the whole of the past comes back to me.'

'Like what?' he asked.

'Don't you remember attacking me when I worked at that little cafe and showed that feller my wedding ring?'

He shook his head. 'No. I don't remember.'

'What about when you kicked and beat me at Wrottesley Road?'

'I don't remember.'

Extraordinary, isn't it? I think it's possible that he really couldn't remember, that his condition was such that those violent and vile acts were wiped away. This is why I am glad to be able to record them now in this book. Because I feel robbed of closure by his death, this book has helped me arrive at conclusions about this crucial figure in my life, and hopefully it will help others in a similar situation do the same.

In a way I feel like the survivor of an epic struggle. He used to crow, 'I'll be around long after you. Or if I die before you, I'll haunt you.' That's funny. He doesn't haunt me, but he left a lot of pain in me and my children.

There may well be other women out there who feel like I do. When he took that knife to me thirty-eight years ago in Joan Crescent and terrified me beyond all reason, he put fear into my heart, and it's there to this day. Some of his violence – beating me when I was pregnant, kicking and punching me – stays with me. I can keep it locked away and at bay, knowing that he can never do it again, but in the back of my head I never want to be in a situation where violence breaks out, because the totality of that fear would come flooding back.

I hate any form of violence, especially emotional. If I see people expressing anger, I feel that fear again. There was one time years ago when I was in a pub in the Old Kent Road with my mother and my brother and somebody tipped a table over and all these glasses shattered. I flew out of the door.

There were a couple of plain-clothes policemen standing in the bar and they came running after me. One of them said, 'It's all right love, it's all right.'

I was trembling. 'Has somebody been glassed?' I whimpered.

'No, not at all,' he said. 'It was a pure accident. Someone knocked into the table.' But the crash sounded so violent to me that I couldn't wait around. I suppose that's the fear that Gerald instilled in me, like the time I went to Benidorm on holiday and truly believed he had gone there to stalk me. These days, the way I deal with that fear is by praying. That consoles me.

There are a lot of men suffering from the same condition as Gerald did, and there is an awful lot of anger out there. Where does it come from? There has to be a cause, and once that is discovered, then the anger can be dealt with and maybe maltreatment of children and women will cease. In this book I have laid some of my demons to rest, and have come to terms with a few others as well. I hope for those of you, particularly women, who are going through rough times, that it has provided some solace and inspiration. Abuse and destructive impulses can be overcome.

I've lost a lot of my family along the way, but there are a few of us still here. My sister Annie, who's seventy-three, swims thirty or forty lengths of a morning. She's like a whirlpool, ever so active, just like Phyllis and Teresa. I reminisce with them often about our days back among the tenements of Wellington Street.

I hope you have enjoyed my story. It has been a long and sometimes rocky road, from racing around the streets of Dublin as a skinny penniless kid to watching George perform on Broadway and at Madison Square Garden; from feeling the shame of nudges and whispers as an unmarried teenage mother to exalting in the love of my family, my gorgeous children and grandchildren. They keep me young.

What's best is this is not the end. There are still adventures to be had, far-off places to see and fascinating people to meet. In fact I'm rather enjoying lying on the bed I made, and crying salty tears no more.

Postscript

A Ghost From the Past

Last September, 2006, just as we were making the final changes to this book, I received an excited call from my sister Phyllis in Dublin.

'You'll never guess what happened just now, Dinah!' she exclaimed. 'The parish priest has been round asking questions about you and Richard.'

Apparently, he had been sent round to enquire as to whether she had a sister called Dinah who had a baby boy way back in 1957. As soon as I heard that, I knew. Seamus. Only he could be behind this.

My sister confirmed that she was related to me and Richard, but what of it? The priest said that a man had approached him and told him he wanted to make contact with me and my son.

'Why would he want to do that?' she asked suspiciously.

'Everyone has a conscience,' said the priest.

'Well it's taken forty-nine years for his to be pricked,' my sister told him.

Anyway, she refused to give my number there and then but said she would consult me. We talked about it and I told her to go ahead.

The following day, a Monday evening, the phone rang. 'Mrs O'Dowd here,' I said.

It was Seamus. The first time I had heard his voice in nearly fifty years, when he disappeared in that puff of smoke which bore him away from any responsibility. One of the first things that struck me was how strong his Dublin accent was.

So, cautiously we asked each other questions. I was blunt: "You're not ill are you?' He said he wasn't.

He said he was fine, and that he had found Richard's birth certificate ten years ago.

'What was on it?' I asked.

'Richard Jude Glynn,' he said.

'Well now it's Richard Jude O'Dowd, and he 's married with three kids,' I explained.

When he told me he had five children, I pointed out that Richard made the tally six. 'Ah yes, yes, I'm sorry,' he said, before asking whether he could speak to Richard.

I took his number and said I would talk to my son. Our son. The one he had neglected for his entire life.

On the Tuesday evening I had a long conversation with Richard, who said that he wanted to at least hear his father's voice. So I gave him the number.

The following night I arrived home late, after darts, and Siobhan said that Richard wanted me to call him urgently. I called and Richard said: 'He's here.'

'Where?' I asked.

'Here in London!'

You could have knocked me down with the proverbial. It seemed that Seamus had spoken to

Richard the night before and then driven to the first available ferry to Liverpool and come all the way down to London.

They had agreed to meet for a meal at City Airport, and had an enjoyable time, though Seamus neither drank or smoked. 'Imagine going out with a Paddy who doesn't drink!' laughed Richard. 'Also, he's got no hair, so I felt pretty proud of my full head at my age.'

As it got late, Richard talked Seamus into staying at a B&B close to him in Blackheath.

'He's only booked in for the one night but wants to stay longer, so we're going to talk to the landlady about putting him up for a few more nights,' enthused Richard.

I was less taken with the whole thing, and had a feeling in my waters.

Even so, I was deeply shocked when Richard told me he had called the B&B the next morning only to be told that Seamus had checked out at 8 am, leaving no message. I could hear how disheartened Richard was when he told me, and I was full of anger.

I gave it a few hours and then called Seamus up, railing at him: 'Is that the best you could do? Give your son a couple of hours after forty-nine years and think that absolves your conscience? This is history repeating itself! You're here and then in a flash you're gone. You call Richard now and tell him you're sorry!'

He was pathetic, stuttering about how he felt he

had to leave. 'So why didn't you call Richard and tell him that, you coward?' I shouted.

I discarded all feelings for this man many years ago and, although angry, I have come to terms with what he has done. But my heart goes out to Richard. He is a lovely chap, who doesn't deserve this. Still, he is reasonable, and doesn't bear his father any ill-will.

In fact we were soon laughing about the episode. Richard's daughter Kelly mispronounces Seamus' name as Shameless – she's just a cockney kid.

And that's what he is to us now.

Shameless.

Daddy's Had A Bad Day

Daddy's had a bad day
He's just a bit uptight
He needs to have a cup of tea
And a bit of peace and quiet

He didn't mean to frighten you
Or say the things he said
And he wasn't trying to punish you
When he sent you up to bed

The thing is Daddy's under lots of pressure
It's been a very stressful time
He had his wages riding on the favourite
And it got beaten on the line

That's why Daddy shouts at Mummy
He's not really being unkind
It's just his way of venting frustration
He says nasty things 'cos it helps him unwind

Mummy isn't crying 'cos Daddy has upset her
She's just feeling sad, Daddy's under so much
    strain
He's out there every day trying to put food on the
    table

Which is hard enough without the three o'clock at
    Chepstow
Being cancelled 'cos of rain

Which is why we all need to be more under-
    standing
And remember Daddy has lots of things to do
Like remembering lots of horses' names
Don't forget; there's more than twenty races to sit
    through

So now you know why Daddy's always angry
It's because of all the things he has to do, for me
    and you
So the next time he comes and slaps you round the
    head
That doesn't mean he doesn't love you

It's probably 'cos you're in his way
He's too tired to tell you: 'You should be in bed'
'Cos Daddy's had a bad day

Kevin O'Dowd